KU-799-920

Painting in England 1540-1620

THE ELIZABETHAN IMAGE

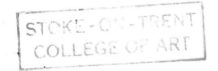
STOKE-ON-TRENT
COLLEGE OF ART

by Roy Strong

AN EXHIBITION ORGANISED BY THE TATE GALLERY 28 NOVEMBER 1969 – 8 FEBRUARY 1970

Catalogue exclusively distributed in USA and Canada by Arno Press, New York

Front Cover ISAAC OLIVER
Edward Herbert, 1st Baron Herbert of Cherbury
circa 1610–15 (no. 142)

Frontispiece MARCUS GHEERAERTS THE YOUNGER
Portrait of Elizabeth I
1592 ? (no. 78)

End-papers (*clothbound edition only*)
Coiling Stems with Stylized Flowers and Spread Eagles
Embroidery design from Thomas Trevelyon's 1608 Miscellany

Back cover **Rose and Crown**
Embroidery design from Thomas Trevelyon's 1608 Miscellany

ACKNOWLEDGEMENTS

APOLLO magazine for the loan of colour plates
used on the front cover
COUNTRY LIFE for the loan of the colour transparency
of 'Sir William Pope' by Robert Peake
THE FOLGER SHAKESPEARE LIBRARY, WASHINGTON DC for permission
to reproduce the embroidery designs
from Thomas Trevelyon's 1608 Miscellany
HER MAJESTY'S STATIONERY OFFICE for the loan of colour plates
for the frontispiece

Published by order of the Trustees 1969

759.2

00299592

Copyright © 1969 The Tate Gallery, London
Catalogue designed and published by the Tate Gallery Publications Department, Millbank, London SW1
Printed in Great Britain by Balding + Mansell, London and Wisbech
Exclusively distributed in USA and Canada by Arno Press, 330 Madison Avenue, New York, NY 10017
Library of Congress Catalogue Card number 72–105938

FOREWORD

NORMAN REID

This is the first of a series of large exhibitions devoted to earlier British painting with which we intend to supplement our more frequent exhibitions of modern art. We decided to inaugurate the series with a show devoted to Elizabethan and Jacobean portraiture and were delighted when Dr Roy Strong agreed to select the works and write the catalogue, on which Mr William Vaughan of the Tate Gallery has also assisted. In fact Dr Strong has gone much further, not only in using his knowledge of the period and of private collections to bring together a splendid group of works, but also in suggesting that the scope of the exhibition should be extended to show something of the cultural background of the period. The special setting for the exhibition has been designed by Mr Christopher Firmstone. Dr Pamela Tudor-Craig has given most useful advice on broken Medieval images for the section on Iconoclasm, and Mr John Harris of the Royal Institute of British Architects has provided the substance of the entries on the Smythson drawings.

A list of lenders to the exhibition is given on page 88. It is a truism to say that without their help this exhibition could never have taken place, but I should like to thank private owners particularly for denuding their walls of such splendidly decorative pictures for so long and for bearing with our many questions about their works. We are particularly indebted to Her Majesty the Queen for lending no fewer than seven works, and the Duke of Bedford and the Executors of the Estate of the late Countess of Suffolk and Berkshire who have lent nine works each. Of public institutions we are particularly indebted to the British Museum, the National Portrait Gallery and the Victoria and Albert Museum.

We have also received some most welcome help with the production of this catalogue. The Paul Mellon Foundation for British Art has paid for the blocks for a number of the colour plates and has been most helpful in supplying photographs made in connection with their publication of Dr Strong's book *The English Icon: Elizabethan and Jacobean Portraiture*. *The Sunday Times Magazine* has generously provided five of the colour transparencies. Other assistance to the catalogue, for which we are also most grateful, is listed opposite.

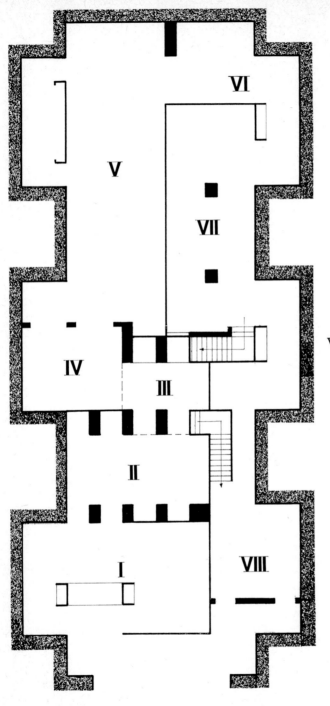

PLAN OF THE EXHIBITION

Exhibition designed by Christopher Firmstone

INTRODUCTION

ROY STRONG This exhibition reconstitutes, for the first time, seventy-five years of English painting from the death of Holbein to the arrival of Van Dyck. Both the exhibition and the catalogue I have conceived in the terms of story telling. It is not enough to attempt to reconstitute the oeuvre of these vanished painters but to place them into the context of their time. Why is there only portraiture? Why do people seem suddenly to be gloomy in the 1590's? Why are the images of Elizabeth I so very peculiar? What did the Elizabethans think about painters and painting? Why, in the new society of Elizabethan and Jacobean England, should there be such an obsession with the trappings of medievalism? To try and answer these questions I have arranged the exhibition in a series of theme rooms followed by galleries. The theme rooms contain material to suggest the thought context to which the paintings belong.

I have deliberately not crammed the catalogue with art historical data on exhibitions, provenance, inscriptions, etc. For all these details the reader is referred to my books *The English Icon: Elizabethan and Jacobean Portraiture* and *Tudor and Jacobean Portraits*, both published this year. All my efforts have been towards giving structural clarity to a period usually thought of as gloomy, obscure and too complicated for anyone except specialist scholars. I hope the exhibition will finally remove this era of painting out of the orbit of antiquarian exploration into that of general appreciation.

I would like to say how much I have enjoyed working with Mr Christopher Firmstone again creating what we hope is an imaginative and evocative spectacle. The staff of the Tate Gallery have borne with patience all the traumas attendant upon presenting a great exhibition. In particular I would like to thank Mr William Vaughan, who has coped with the brunt of the organising. For the catalogue, which captures so well the mood of the exhibition, I am indebted to Mr Brian Rushton. To my colleague, Mr Norman Reid, I owe the debt of materialising a longed-for dream of resurrecting a lost century of English painting.

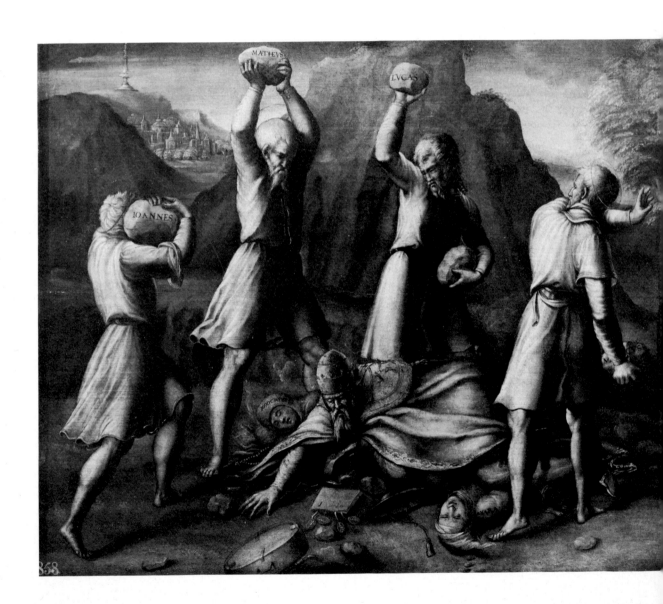

IOANNES   MATTEVS   LVCAS

Art and Anti-Art

I

'Under a minor prince, and amidst a
struggle of religions, we are not likely to
meet with much account of the arts'

HORACE WALPOLE

757·

irolamo da Treviso *The Four Evangelists stoning the Pope* (no. 7)

The Monarchs

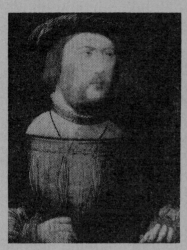

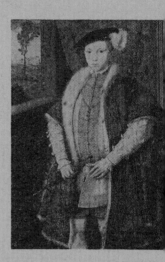

1
ARTIST UNKNOWN
Henry VIII

The National Portrait Gallery
Oil on panel, 23 × 17½ inches

Henry VIII was the only member of the Tudor dynasty who was a major patron of the visual arts. During the early part of his reign the prime patron was Cardinal Wolsey and the King's activities had centred on lavish court spectacles of which the Field of the Cloth of Gold in 1520 was the most famous. These were chivalrous fêtes mainly in emulation of the court of Burgundy. With the Reformation, however, the emphasis changed. Wolsey fell from power and the King took over both his palaces, Hampton Court and York Place, soon to be Whitehall. During the 1530's the Crown, supplemented by a vast influx of wealth from ecclesiastical confiscations, embarked on a major artistic programme. Further building took place at Hampton Court while York Place was transformed at enormous speed into the vast complex of Whitehall which was finished enough by 1533 to receive Anne Boleyn as Queen. In 1538 Henry began Nonsuch which again was built at great speed. By the close of the thirties the renaissance in the visual arts seems quite definitely to be coming via France. Nonsuch was directly inspired by Fontainebleau and Nicolò da Modena, who had worked there, carried out the plaster decoration.

This portrait is a typical workshop image of the King produced in the late 30's or early 40's. By then portraits of the reigning monarch were in demand for domestic consumption.

2
CIRCLE OF SCROTS
Edward VI *circa* 1546–47

Her Majesty the Queen
Oil on panel, 42¼ × 32¼ inches

Edward VI was nine when he came to the throne and fifteen when he died. He inherited from his father a passion for pageantry and military spectacles but during his reign all major patronage by the Crown ceased. During the first part of the reign his uncle, Edward Seymour, Duke of Somerset was Lord Protector. He fell from power in 1550 and was succeeded by the unscrupulous Duke of Northumberland, who persuaded Edward to will the crown to Lady Jane Grey, Northumberland's daughter-in-law. During Edward's reign major religious reform was carried through, the Crown was despoiled of many of the assets it had acquired by Henry VIII's confiscations and inflation and rural change led to uprisings in East Anglia and the South-west.

This portrait of Edward (and one of Elizabeth as a Princess) are both the work of the same painter. Edward's was painted shortly before his accession on January 28th 1547 as he wears the Prince of Wales's feathers as a jewel. The technique of the painting is definitely Flemish and the picture should be by William Scrots, Holbein's successor as King's Painter. The attribution as the evidence now stands is difficult to maintain as our knowledge of Scrots' work is so fragmentary.

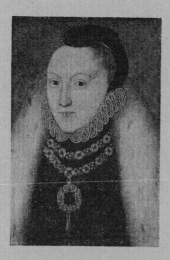

3
ARTIST UNKNOWN after ANTONIO MOR

Mary I probably late 16th Century

Her Majesty The Queen
Oil on panel, 36¾ × 29⅞ inches

Mary succeeded Edward on a wave of popularity and reaction. She married Philip of Spain in 1554 and reconciled England to Rome. Later there followed an unpopular persecution of Protestants and a war with France which resulted in the loss of Calais. During her reign the restoration of order in government administration began after the disastrous reign of Edward. Although she inherited her father's passion for splendour and magnificence, she was not a person of great visual taste.

The portrait is a derivation, probably late 16th century in date, of Mor's portrait of 1554 (no. 35).

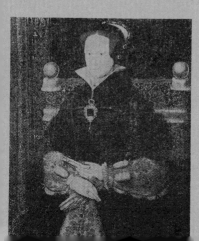

4
ARTIST UNKNOWN

Elizabeth I *circa* 1560

The National Portrait Gallery
Oil on panel, 15½ × 10¾ inches

When Elizabeth succeeded Mary in November 1558 England's fortunes were low and the first decade of Elizabeth's reign should be viewed as a continuation of the troubled middle years of the century. Once again England went Protestant, although Elizabeth and her chief minister, William Cecil, later Lord Burghley, pursued a cautious, ambiguous policy. The defeat of the Northern Rebellion of 1569, in which the great Catholic magnates of the north tried to topple Cecil from the Council, and the papal excommunication of 1570 meant the end of an era. No major artistic projects were launched by the Crown during this unsettled period.

An example of one of the very early portraits of the Queen in her late twenties. In 1567 the Earl of Sussex told Margaret of Parma, Regent of the Netherlands 'that the picture commonly made to be solde did nothinge resemble . . . for that it was drawne in blacke with a hoode and a cornet which the Queen no longer wore'.

Great were the difficulties surrounding the production of adequate likenesses of the new Queen. Hans Eworth, Mary Tudor's court painter, was abandoned and no satisfactory painter was found until the emergence of Nicholas Hilliard at the opening of the seventies. In 1563 the Queen's councillors were driven to the extreme of drafting a proclamation forbidding the manufacture of further portraits until 'some speciall person . . . shall have first fynished a portraiture thereof, after which fynished, her majesty will be content that all other payntors, or gravers . . . shall and maye at ther plesurs follow the said patron (pattern) or first portraiture'.

This gives a specific insight into the method of producing the Queen's image and although hundreds of portraits of her exist they nearly all conform to one or other of about six face patterns. Elizabeth obviously took a considerable interest in her own portraiture and there seems to have been a tacit understanding that accessories in each should vary. As late as 1596 the Privy Council ordered the destruction of unseemly portraits which caused the Queen 'great offence'.

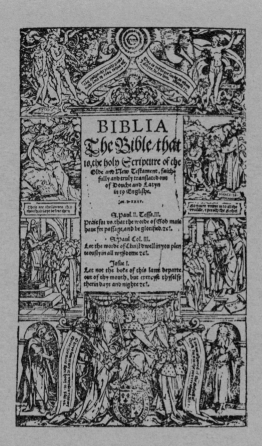

THE GOVERNOVR.

Kynge Philippis wordes to Alexãder.

¶ Kynge Philip, whan he harde that his sonne Alexander dydde synge swetely and propzely, rebuked hym gentylly, sayinge, But Alexander, be ye not ashamed, that ye can synge so well and connyngly? wherby he mente, that the open profession of that craft was but of a base estimation. And that it suffysed a noble man, hauing therin knowlege, eyther to vse it secretelye, for the refreshynge of his wytte, whan he hath tyme of solace: orels onely herynge the contention of noble musicyens, to gyue iugement in the excellêcie of theyr connynges. These be the causes, wherunto hauyng regarde, musyke is not onely tollerable, but also cõmendable. For as Aristotle sayth: Musike in the olde tyme was nombzed amonge sciences, for as moche as nature seketh not onely, howe to be in busynes well occupyed, but also howe in quyetnes to be commendably dysposed.

Musyke pzofitable.

¶ And if the childe be of a perfect inclinatiõ and towardnes to vertue, and very aptly dysposed to this science, and rypely doth vnderstand the reason and concozdance of tunes, the tutozs office shal be, to persuade hym, to haue pzincipally in remembzaunce his astate, which maketh hym exempt from the lybertie of vsynge this science in euery tyme and place: that is to say, that it onely serueth

THE FYRSTE BOKE. 23

serueth for recreation, after tedious oz laborious affaires. And to shewe hym, that a gentylman playinge oz syngynge in a commune adyence, appayzeth his estimation: The people forgettynge reuerence, whan they beholde him in symilitude of a cõmon seruaunt oz mynstrel. Yet notwithstanding, he shal commende the perfecte vnderstandynge of musyke, declarynge howe necessary it is for the better attaynng the knowlege of a publyke weale. which as I before sayd, is made of an ozdre of astates and degrees, and by reason therof conteyneth in it a perfect harmony: whiche he shall afterwarde moze perfectly vnderstand, whan he shal happe to rede the bokes of Plato and Aristo. of publike weales: wherin be wzitten dyuers examples of musyke and gemetry. In this fourme may a wise and cyrcuspecte tutoz, adapte the pleasant science of musike to a necessary z laudable purpose.

That it is cõmendable in a gentylman to paint and kerue exactly, if nature ther to doth induce hym. Cap. viii.

If the chylde be of nature inclyned (as many haue ben) to peynte with a pen, oz to fourme images in stoone oz tree: he shulde not be therfrom withdrawen, oz nature

5

SIR THOMAS ELYOT

The Boke named The Governour 1537 (first edition 1531)

The British Museum Library

Sir Thomas Elyot (1490 ?–1546), diplomatist and author, rose under the powerful patronage of Thomas Cromwell. Later he was ambassador to Charles V. He published *The Boke named The Governour* in 1531 dedicating it to Henry VIII. It is a typical renaissance treatise on the fashioning of statesmen for service to the Crown, but it contains an important chapter — 'That it is commendable in a gentilman to paint and kerve exactly if nature therto doth induce him'. Painters and sculptors were regarded as tradesmen and Elyot's view was an *avant garde* one. He justifies it by appeals to Roman Emperors, to the use of drawing in war and to its value in encouraging virtue by depicting moral *exempla*. Even then, he admits, it should only be 'as a secrete pastime, or recreation of the wittes'. It took almost a century for these ideas to be accepted by a literate aristocracy and gentry.

6

The Bible that is the holy Scripture of the Olde and New Testament, faithfully and truly translated . . . 1536

The British Museum Library

The first official translation of the Bible into English by Miles Coverdale was brought out under the powerful patronage of Thomas Cromwell. Holbein was in the service of the latter in the 1530's and produced, in addition to this title page, antipapal woodcuts. The vision here of the Monarch enthroned, clasping the sword of Justice and delivering the Bible to his people was a definitive one for both Tudors and Stuarts. While churches were emptied of religious images they were filled with symbols of royal power in the form of the royal arms put up over the chancel arch and books issued by royal authority. In the dedication the King is lauded as 'in this world present, the person of God . . . he only under God is the chief head of all the congregation and church of the same'.

7
GIROLAMO DA TREVISO

The Four Evangelists stoning the Pope *circa* 1536

Her Majesty The Queen
Oil on panel, 27 × 33 inches
Illustrated on page 8

During the anti-papal and anti-clerical campaigns of the 1530's paintings of this sort found favour at court. This is one of a series of anti-papal paintings recorded in Henry VIII's collection in 1542. Others showed Truth unveiling the iniquities of the Pope and Henry VIII wielding a sword, inscribed *Verbum Dei*, trampling on the Pope as the Beast of the Apocalypse. In this picture, a unique survival, the true light of the Gospel, symbolised by the candle, triumphs over the falsehood of Rome. The Pope and his accomplices, Hypocrisy and Avarice, are vanquished by the Evangelists. Beneath the Pope can be seen a cardinal's hat, indulgences, a holy water stoop and a rosary. The composition is based on a woodcut in the 1536 Bible depicting the stoning of the blasphemous man. Girolamo da Treviso was one of a number of Italian artists who found service with Henry VIII.

8
GERLACH FLICKE

Thomas Cranmer 1546

The National Portrait Gallery
Oil on panel, 38¾ × 30 inches

Cranmer (1489–1556) became Archbishop of Canterbury in 1533 and dissolved Henry's marriage to Catherine of Aragon. Under Edward VI he carried through major religious reforms, supervising the First and Second Edwardian Prayer Books, of 1549 and 1552. Under Mary he was imprisoned, degraded and burned. It fell to him as Archbishop to implement the iconoclast policy ordered by the Council under Edward.

Signed. The earliest known portrait by Flicke. It betrays the influence of Holbein's *Archbishop Warham*, near to which it must originally have hung at Lambeth Palace. He is shown in reforming vein reading the Pauline Epistles with a book on faith and works nearby.

9
ARTIST UNKNOWN

Edward VI and The Pope *circa* 1548

The National Portrait Gallery
Oil on panel, 24½ × 35⅜ inches

An anti-papal allegory probably painted shortly after February 1548 when Archbishop Cranmer, in accordance with the decisions of the Council, ordered the destruction of all religious images. In the background, top right, soldiers smash statues of saints and haul down an image of the Virgin and Child. The ruins collapsing in flames in the distance probably allude to vanquished Rome as the wicked Babylon. Edward VI triumphs over the Pope by the Bible: THE WORDE OF THE LORD ENDURETH FOR EVER. The *infulae* of the Pope's tiara are labelled *Idolatry* and *Superstition* and the front of his alb *All flesh is grass*. Nearby is a further inscription *Fained Holiness*. To the left a Franciscan and Dominican friar attempt to topple the royal dais. Henry VIII on his deathbed gestures to his successor while to Edward's left is Somerset and below the Council, Northumberland, Cranmer and Bedford.

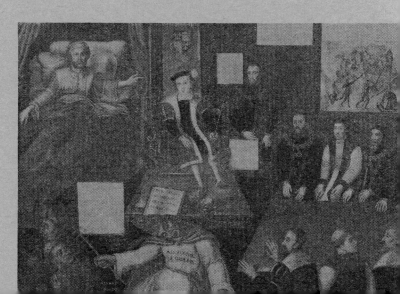

BROKEN IMAGES
These examples are included to
show the appalling destruction
that overtook English medieval art
during the Reformation iconoclast
campaigns.

10

Order of the Privy Council for the Removal of Images
February 21st 1548

Cranmer's Register, Lambeth Palace Library
Photocopy

On February 21st 1548 the Council wrote to Archbishop
Cranmer informing him of their decision in favour of the
removal of all images from churches. Somerset and the Council
ordered him to implement this in his own diocese and instruct
his fellow bishops to follow in their own sees. All rich shrines
and the plate that went with them were confiscated by the
Crown. Already in 1538 shrines which had been centres of
pilgrimage had been suppressed, but this time there was to be a
wholesale destruction of English medieval art as everything that
could be construed as an image was hacked to pieces.
Inevitably, the effectiveness with which this was carried out
varied throughout the country. The result was the abrupt end
of an industry made up of painters, sculptors, embroiderers,
gold and silver-smiths who produced objects associated with
pre-Reformation Catholic ritual.

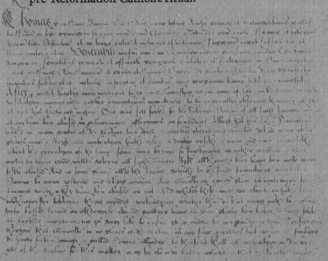

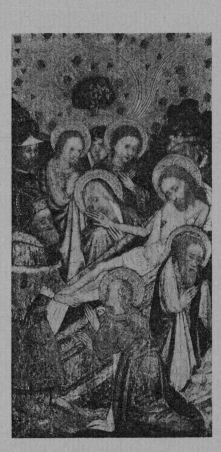

11 (right)
EAST ANGLIAN SCHOOL Early 15th Century

The Entombment

Ipswich Museums and Art Galleries
Oil on panel, 37 × 18¼ inches

Despite recent restoration, scars made by iconoclasts on the
faces are still visible.

ARTISTS UNKNOWN

12

Head 15th Century

The Parochial Church Council of St. Cuthbert, Wells
Alabaster, 12 × 8 × 5 inches

12a

Head 15th Century

The Parochial Church Council of St. Cuthbert, Wells
Alabaster, 12 × 8 × 5 inches

13

The Virgin Mary Early 15th Century

The Parochial Church Council of St. Michael Coslany Church,
Norwich
On loan to Norwich Museums
Stone, $22\frac{1}{2}$ × $8\frac{1}{2}$ × $8\frac{1}{2}$ inches

14

The Archangel Michael Early 15th Century

The Parochial Church Council of St. Michael Coslany Church,
Norwich
On loan to Norwich Museums
Stone, 25 × 10 × 10 inches

15

Headless figure 15th Century

The Dean and Chapter of Winchester Cathedral
Stone, 36 × 15 × 15 inches

16

Head of Christ 15th Century

The Dean and Chapter of Winchester Cathedral
Stone, 15 × 10 × 10 inches

17

Head of a Pope 15th Century

The Dean and Chapter of Winchester Cathedral
Stone, 12 × 8 × 8 inches

18

Head of a Queen 15th Century

The Dean and Chapter of Winchester Cathedral
Stone, 15 × 12 × 12 inches

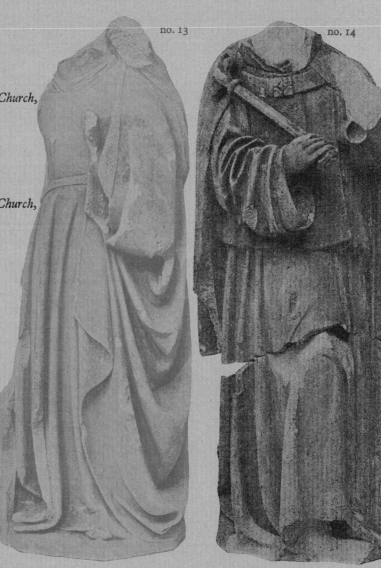

no. 13   no. 14

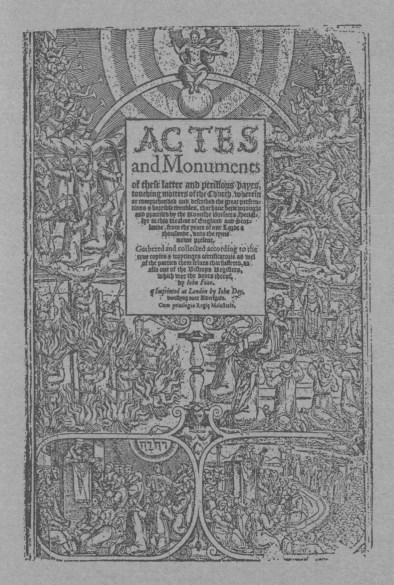

19

A Proclamation against breakying or defacing monuments or antiquities 1560

The British Museum Library

Under Mary images were re-erected within churches but soon after Elizabeth's accession mob iconoclasm broke out. Throughout the summer and autumn of 1559 public bonfires of roods, images and other catholic liturgical items took place. By 1560 this had got so out of hand that tombs and glass windows were being destroyed. The result was a proclamation forbidding 'the breaking or defacing of any parcel of any Monument, or tomb, or grave, or other inscription . . . or to breake any image of kings, princes, or nobles estates of this realm, or any other'.

Elizabeth herself took a middle way on images, keeping, to the horror of her bishops, a crucifix in her chapel. The official Anglican statement on images in Jewel's *Apology* (1562) is also moderate as it does not deny their value in teaching the illiterate but argues that it is safer to remove them least they lead to idolatry.

20

JOHN FOXE

Actes and Monuments 1563

The British Museum Library

Foxe's *Book of Martyrs* appeared first in English in 1563. This vast compilation frames the sufferings of English Protestant Martyrs under Mary within a framework of human history based on the concept of the Four Monarchies as related in an exposition of the mystical numbers of the Apocalypse revealed in a vision to Foxe. It was a book of immense influence, Convocation in 1570 ruling that copies of it should be placed in cathedral churches, in the houses of archbishops and other dignitaries. The main theme is the endless struggle of Christ and Antichrist, reflected in the battle of the Emperor versus the Pope, now devolved upon sovereigns in their own 'empires'. This story was vividly brought to life by a series of woodcuts which must have been familiar to most Elizabethans. In these the Pope forces the Emperor Henry IV and his family to wait barefoot in the snow, Alexander III treads on the neck of Frederick Barbarossa and King John is poisoned by the monk of Swinehead. Now all this has been reversed and Henry VIII is shown trampling the Pope underfoot.

II

Hans Eworth and his Contemporaries

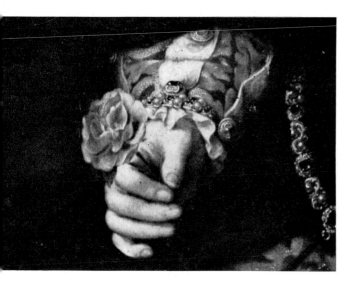

Antonio Moro: detail from *Mary I* (no. 35)

Vivre pour mourire,
Mourire pour vivre,

INSCRIPTION ON A PORTRAIT BY HANS EWORTH 1557 (NO. 31)

JOHN BETTES I flourished 1530–before 1576

Bettes is the only artist who, on grounds of style, was probably trained and worked in the studio of Holbein. The *Unknown Man* (no. 21) of 1545 is the only certain work by him and other portraits that can be attributed are close to this date. They are *Sir William Butts the Younger* (154?: Boston Museum of Fine Arts); *Thomas, 1st Baron Wentworth* (1549: National Portrait Gallery) (no. 22) and *Sir William Cavendish* (circa 1545: National Trust, Hardwick Hall). All his work is of an extremely high quality very close to Holbein, for instance, in tricks such as the delineation of the thickness of an eyelid. He inherits too a blatant frankness in recording the characters of his sitters.

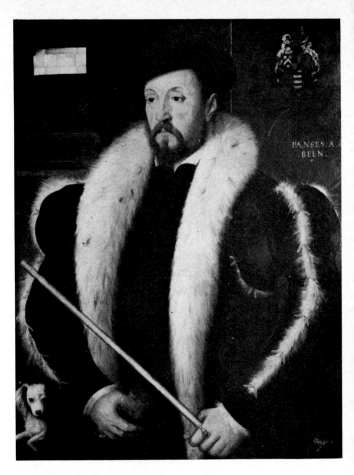

22 (above, before restoration)

Thomas Wentworth, 1st Baron Wentworth of Nettlestead 1549

The National Portrait Gallery
Oil on panel, $30\frac{3}{8} \times 28\frac{7}{8}$ inches

Attributed. X-ray shows that Wentworth became Lord Chamberlain during the painting of this portrait. He was appointed in February 1549–50 with the consequence that his new white rod of office was inserted into one hand and the gloves they were holding were placed in his other.

Lord Wentworth (1501–1551) served in the household of Henry VIII's sister Mary. Later he supported the Reformation and was one of the peers who tried and condemned Anne Boleyn. He became Lord Chamberlain of the household under Edward VI

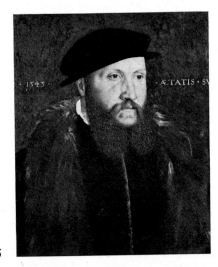

21

Unknown man 1545

The Tate Gallery
Oil on panel, $18\frac{1}{2} \times 16\frac{1}{8}$ inches

Inscribed on the reverse of the panel: *faict par Jehan Bettes Anglois*. The portrait has been reduced in size and was probably closer in proportion to no. 22 at one time.

WILLIAM SCROTS flourished 1537–1553/4

Scrots, who had been court painter to Mary of Hungary, Regent of the Netherlands, came to England in the autumn of 1545. He was the official successor to Holbein, being in receipt of a very high salary until he left England or died in 1553/4. Scrots is one of the most puzzling painters dealt with in this exhibition and we are nowhere near to unravelling his *oeuvre*. The pictures for which we have evidence of one sort or another are variable in quality and often studio pieces. We can be sure, however, that it is he who is responsible for the introduction into England of the glossy style of courtly mannerism evolved in Florence in the late thirties and forties. Under his influence interest in a sitter's character recedes and is replaced by a metallic rendering of lavish accessories.

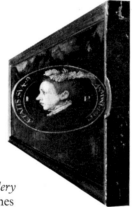

23

Edward VI 1546

The National Portrait Gallery
Oil on panel, $16\frac{3}{4} \times 63$ inches

Formerly signed. Vertue records in 1713 that the frame of this picture was signed: *Guilhelmus pingebat*. The landscapes in the spandrels are a later, probably 17th century, addition. Throughout the late 16th and early 17th century this portrait or anamorphosis, to use the proper technical term, was shown to every official tourist visiting Whitehall Palace. Apparently it had some special viewing device attached to it which enabled the King's head to be seen in proper perspective. This type of visual trick had been used earlier in England by Holbein in his *Ambassadors* (1533). The attitude to perspective as a 'device' is very typical of the entire period:

> Her lookes were like the pictures that are made,
> To th'optike reason; one way like a shade;
> Another monster like, and every way
> To passers by, and such as made no stay,
> To view her in a right line, face to face.
>
> (GEORGE CHAPMAN *Eugenia*)

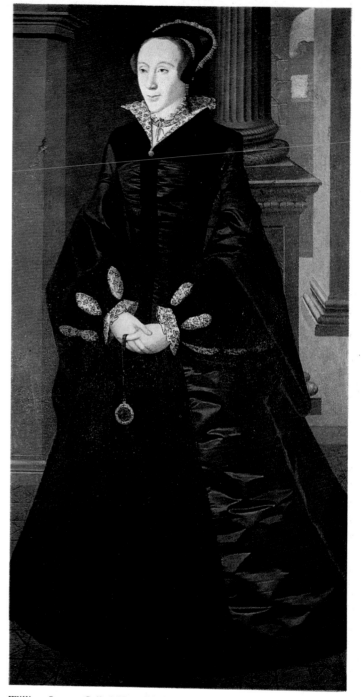

William Scrots: Called *Mary I* (no. 26)

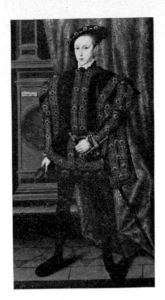

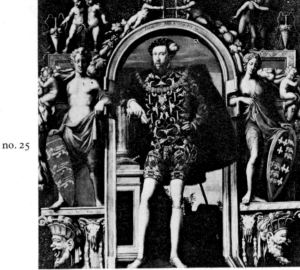

no. 25

24

Edward VI *circa* 1550

Her Majesty The Queen
Oil on panel, 65¾ × 35¾ inches

This is the best of a number of full-length portraits of
Edward VI, all more or less identical except for the costume.
They can be documented as being by Scrots or from his studio
by a payment in March 1551/2 to the artist for 'three great
tables' (i.e. panel pictures), two of which were of Edward. Both
the latter had been sent to ambassadors abroad, one to Sir John
Mason, ambassador in France. Two versions of the picture are
in France, one in the Louvre and one at Rouanne, which further
corroborates the documentation. Classical architecture with
rich coloured marbles occur in a number of pictures we can
associate with Scrots. The pose is based on Holbein's portrait
of Henry VIII in the lost wall painting in the Privy Chamber
in Whitehall Palace. Scrots' was probably inspired by full
lengths of the Habsburg archdukes that Seisenegger produced
very close in concept to this.

A great many versions of the portrait of Edward exist of varying
sizes produced through the 16th and into the 17th century.
In all of them the faulty drawing of the left ear is perpetuated.

25

Henry Howard, Earl of Surrey *circa* 1550

The Duke of Norfolk
Oil on canvas, 87½ × 86½ inches

This is an excellent instance of the complexities attendant upon
the study of early English painting. We know that one of the
three 'great tables' paid for in 1551/2 was of Surrey (see no. 24),

and Scrots has therefore been associated with the various
versions that exist of the present picture, of which this one is
generally accepted as being the earliest. The payment,
however, is for a full length on wood not canvas and I am
inclined to the view that all the various versions of this portrait
of Surrey, including this one, are copies after a lost original by
Scrots. The composition is certainly right for him with its
classical ruins against which Surrey leans wearily in a portrait
formula of a type ultimately derived from Northern Italy and
Moretto.

Henry Howard, Earl of Surrey (1517?–1547) was the eldest
son of the 3rd Duke of Norfolk. With his father a victim of
Hertford, both Norfolk and Surrey being sent to the Tower in
1546. He was executed on a trumped-up charge of quartering
his own arms with the royal arms. With Wyatt he introduced the
English court to the poetic traditions of the Italian renaissance,
particularly the cult of Petrarch.

26

Called **Mary I** *circa* 1550

Captain R. E. Huddleston
Oil on panel, 80 × 44 inches
Illustrated in colour on page 19

Attributed. Notice the classical architecture in the background
and the glossy rendering of the silks that connects it with
no. 24.

MASTER JOHN flourished 1544

Anonymous master recorded in the Privy Purse expenses of the Princess Mary Tudor. A painter of grand patronage with an extremely idiosyncratic style. He develops the hieratic tendencies inherent in Holbein's final late manner, producing formalised icons anticipating by forty years the bejewelled abstractions of Elizabeth I. Painting over gold leaf is one of his characteristic techniques.

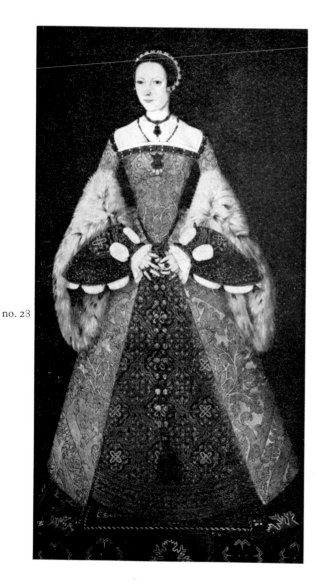

no. 23

27

Mary I 1544

The National Portrait Gallery
Oil on panel, 28 × 20 inches

Documented. Presumably identical with the picture paid for in November 1544: *Item, paid to one John that drue her grace in a table, v.li.* The portrait was probably once in the possession of Sir Richard Pexall, Master of the Buckhounds when she was Queen. His daughter married Bernard Brocas in whose family it descended. The jewel at her breast may be identical with one sent her by her father in 1542 'A flowre with fyve great Diamondes, ij. Rubies, oon Emeraurde, and a great pearle pendaunte'. The portrait is exhibited here for the first time in its cleaned and restored state.

28

Lady Jane Grey *circa* 1545

The National Portrait Gallery
Oil on panel, 71 × 37 inches

Attributed. Formerly wrongly identified as Catherine Parr, its correct identity was established through the jewel she wears at her breast. This appears in the earliest certain portrait of Jane Grey, an engraving in the *Herωologia* (1620). The portrait is clearly influenced in its formula by Holbein's *Christina, Duchess of Milan*.

Lady Jane Grey (1537–1554) was daughter of Henry Grey, Duke of Suffolk and grand-daughter of Henry VIII's sister Mary. A notable bluestocking she was the victim of her father-in-law, Northumberland's ambition. Willed the crown by her cousin Edward, she was Queen for ten days. Mary executed her after Wyatt's rebellion.

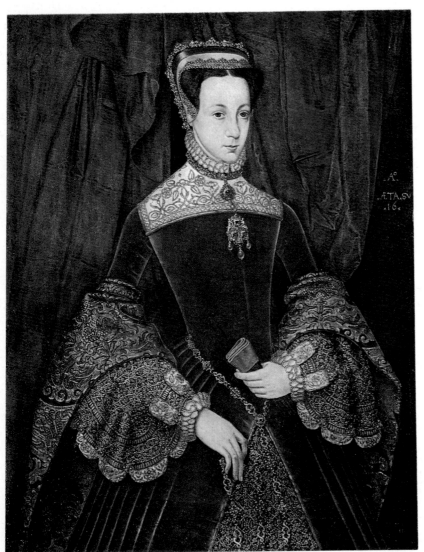

HANS EWORTH flourished 1540–1573

Hans Eworth is the most important artist of quality working in England in the mid-16th century. Very little is known about him due to the extraordinary transformations his name is liable to undergo. He is probably identical with a Jan Euworts listed as a freeman of the Antwerp Guild of St. Luke in 1540. The earliest of a whole series of pictures bearing his monogram HE is dated 1549. Under Mary I he became her official portraitist but was not patronised, apparently, by the young Elizabeth I until 1572 when he was commissioned to design costumes and décor for court fêtes. Many of Eworth's sitters connect him with the Catholic circle of Mary Tudor. His style was basically modelled on that of Jan van Scorel, but he was subsequently influenced by Holbein and later Clouet. Twenty-six pictures are either signed or documented as being by him; nine more can be accepted with confidence. His work makes up the most complete *oeuvre* of any mid-Tudor artist. Because of the exhibition *Hans Eworth and his Circle* (National Portrait Gallery, 1965) he is deliberately under-represented in this exhibition. We have, however, included his masterpiece *Frances Brandon, Duchess of Suffolk and Adrian Stokes* (no. 33). No other painter resident in England during this period approaches Eworth in the delicate observation of human character.

no. 30

29

Sir John Luttrell 1550

The Courtauld Institute of Art
Oil on panel, 43½ × 33 inches

Formerly signed. One of the strangest of all Tudor pictures.
A copy made in 1591 for the sitter's nephew includes all the
inscriptions intact and the monogram (Trustees of
G. F. Luttrell). The allegory alludes to the Treaty of Peace
made by Warwick (later Northumberland) in 1550. It is
important as the most striking instance of the direct influence
of the School of Fontainebleau on English art, and indeed it has
been argued that the inset allegorical scene is by a second
painter.

Sir John Luttrell (1518 ?–1551) was a soldier and trader, who
fought in the Scottish campaign of 1547, but died four years
later at Woolwich of a fever while preparing for an expedition
to Morocco. The allegory has been studied in detail by
Frances A. Yates: the central figure in the vision is Peace.
To the right Venus curbs the wrath of war, symbolised by the
horse, which she bridles with a bit. Behind these seem to be
Minerva and the Graces personifying the fruits of peace. To the
left of Peace two ladies embrace alluding to *Amicitia*, one having
a purse in her hand referring to the money paid by Henry II to
Edward VI for Boulogne. Sir John is depicted as a fighting sea
divinity rescued from the storms of war by *Pax*. The actual
allusions in the storm-tossed ship still elude us although it
clearly refers in a general way to the recent war.

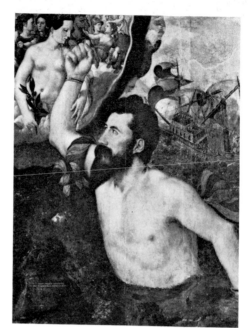

no. 29

30

? Mary FitzAlan, Duchess of Norfolk ? 1555

Private collection
Oil on panel, 35 × 28 inches

Documented. Exhibited for the first time since cleaning and
restoration. The portrait is almost certainly identical with that
recorded in the Lumley Inventory of 1590: *Of Mary Duches of
Northfolke, daughter to the last Earl of Arundele (Fitzallen)
doone by Haunce*. It is first recorded in the Hamilton collection
in 1704: *A picture of the Dutches of Norfolk in Queen
Elizabeth's time down to the knees*. The portrait has been cut
down slightly and the existing inscriptions must be copies of
those on amputated parts of the picture. These include the H E
monogram bottom right and the impossible date 1565. This
must, on grounds of costume, be a mis-transcript for 1555.

Mary FitzAlan (1540–1557) was daughter of the last Earl of
Arundel. She married Norfolk in 1555 and died in childbed
aged seventeen.

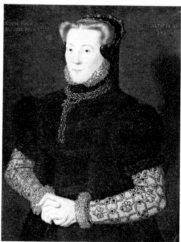

31

Unknown Lady 1557

The Tate Gallery
Oil on panel, 23½ × 19 inches

Signed. A typical example of one of Eworth's slightly less than
life-scale portraits. Probably there was once a companion
portrait of her husband. The sad motto, a remembrance of
death, is typical throughout this period: *VIVRE POVR
MOVRIR, MOVRIR POVR VIVRE.*

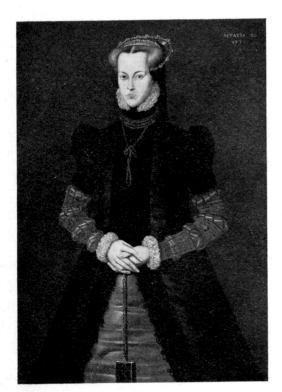

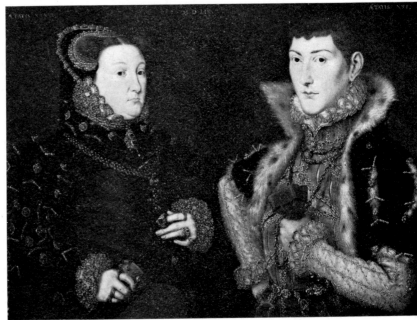

Frances Brandon, Duchess of Suffolk and Adrian Stokes 1559

32

Anne, Lady Penruddocke 1557

Private collection
Oil on panel, 42 × 31 inches

Attributed. Although much damaged this is undoubtedly by Eworth, possibly once even signed. It is the first time that it has been exhibited as Eworth's work. Lady Penruddocke was the second wife of Sir George Penruddocke (died 1601) of Ivy Church, Wiltshire. He was standard-bearer to the Earl of Pembroke at the battle of St. Quentin, 1557.

Colonel J. C. Wynne-Finch
Oil on panel, 19¾ × 27 inches

Signed. Eworth's masterpiece. Frances Brandon (1517–1559) was the daughter of Charles Brandon, Duke of Suffolk by the Princess Mary, Henry VIII's sister. She was mother of Lady Jane Grey and Catherine Grey. Frances married Charles Brandon in 1533 but he was executed in 1554 for his part in the Wyatt rebellion. She married Adrian Stokes, her secretary and groom of the chamber, not long after, he being sixteen years her junior. Elizabeth I remarked 'Has the woman so far forgotten herself as to marry a common groom!'

GERLACH FLICKE died 1558

Painter from Osnabruck of somewhat limited talent who worked in England *circa* 1546 till his death. Even during this short time he was imprisoned and paid a visit abroad.

THOMAS CRANMER, 1546 (see no. 8).

ANTONIO MOR 1517/20–1576/7

Flemish artist of immense influence in defining the mannerist portrait for the northern courts. He worked for the Habsburg court both in the Low Countries and in Spain. According to van Mander he was sent to England to paint Mary I as prospective bride of Philip of Spain. There is no English evidence for this visit, but he did come and paint Mary from life and had a considerable influence on English painting in the sixties. Sir Henry Lee, for instance, sat for this portrait when he passed through the Low Countries in 1568 (see no. 54).

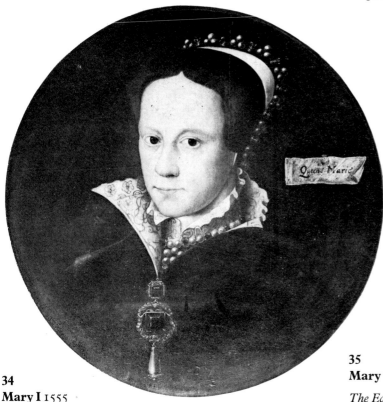

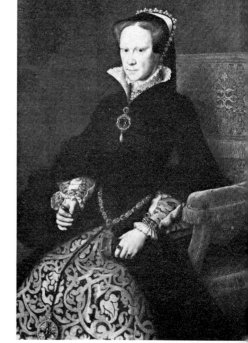

34
Mary I 1555

Durham College, Cathedral Library
Oil on panel, $17\frac{1}{4}$ inches diameter

Documented. The portrait bears a *cartellino* of the type painted on many of the pictures belonging to John, Lord Lumley (see, e.g., nos. 36, 38, 39, 57). It is recorded in the Lumley Inventory of 1590: *Of Queen Mary drawne by Garlick*. The portrait is based on that by Antonio Mor painted the year before (see no. 35).

35
Mary I 1554

The Earl Compton
Oil on panel, 45 × 33 inches

Signed. One of the three certain versions by Mor. The pattern was multiplied and copied by native artists (see nos. 3 and 34). As there is no evidence on the English side, it is possible that Mor came over in the train of Philip. The portrait epitomises a penetrating directness of characterisation that was not to find favour with Mary's sister, Elizabeth I.

SIR HENRY LEE, 1568 (see no. 54).

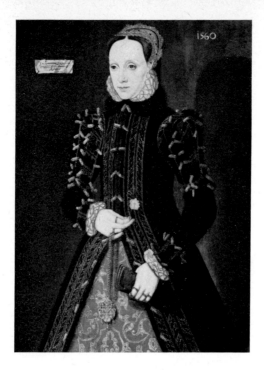

STEVEN VAN DER MUELEN flourished 1543–68

Antwerp artist trained under Willem van Cleve who worked in London throughout the sixties. During this period he gave the English court a version of Antonio Mor's style, realistic, shadowed and rather ponderous. He is referred to in the Lumley Inventory of 1590 as 'the famous paynter Steven' and Elizabeth I sent him to paint a prospective bridegroom, Eric XIV of Sweden. This exhibition is the first time any attempt has been made to reconstitute his *oeuvre*. About twenty-four pictures have so far emerged as possibly by him, two of which are definitely documented and four of which may relate to documentation.

36
Elizabeth FitzGerald, Countess of Lincoln 1560

J. B. Gold, Esq.
Oil on panel, 36 × 29 inches

Attributed. Elizabeth FitzGerald (*c.* 1528–1589) youngest daughter of the 9th Earl of Kildare married firstly Sir Anthony Browne and secondly Edward Fiennes, Earl of Lincoln. She used to be identified as 'the fair Geraldine' of Surrey's poems. A year after this picture was painted Archbishop Parker wrote to Sir William Cecil that in his opinion the Countess ought to be chastised in Bridewell. The portrait is recorded in the Lumley Inventory of 1590: *Of the Countess of Lincolne, daughter to the Earle of Kildare.*

37 (right)
Eric XIV 1561

National Museum, Stockholm
Oil on canvas, 74 × 40 inches

Documented. In 1561 Steven travelled in the train of an English merchant, John Dymoch, to Sweden to paint Eric XIV as prospective bridegroom of Elizabeth I. The portrait was painted in March and the King was so pleased with it that he gave the artist a reward of 100 daler. No history is known of this portrait until it appeared in the London art trade in 1932.

Eric XIV (1533–77), King of Sweden, reigned from 1561 to 1568. His rule was marked by a savage suppression of the nobility, who rose and deposed him in 1568.

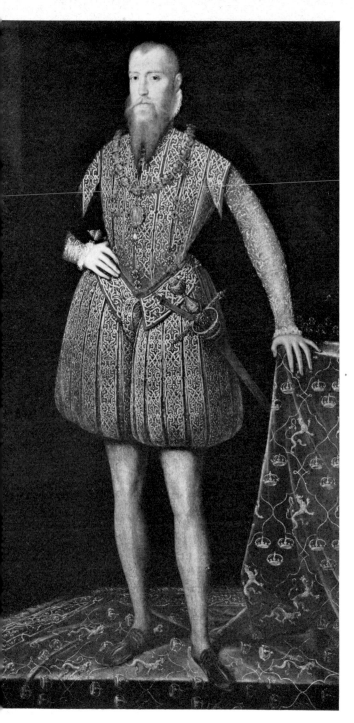

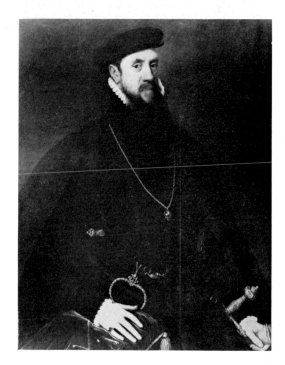

38 (above)

Henry FitzAlan, Earl of Arundel 1562

The Earl of Carlisle
Oil on panel, 43¾ × 33½ inches

Possibly documented. At least three versions of this portrait exist, one of which, and almost certainly this one, should be identical with that recorded in the Lumley Inventory of 1590: *of the last Earle of Arundell Fitzallen, drawne twise by the famous paynter Steven.*

Henry FitzAlan, Earl of Arundel (1511 ?–80) was Henry VIII's Lord Chamberlain from 1544. Although he fell victim to Northumberland in Edward's reign, his double dealing brought about the succession of Mary, to whom he delivered the great seal. She made him Lord Steward of the Household and he continued in favour under Elizabeth, chiefly on account of his immense power as leader of the old catholic nobility. Finally fell from power over complicity in the Ridolfi Plot. He was 'stronge of bone, furnished with cleane and firm fleshe, voide of fogines and fatness'. He probably owned the Holbein Cartoon of Henry VIII and the Holbein drawings now at Windsor.

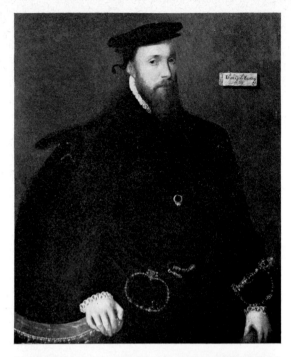

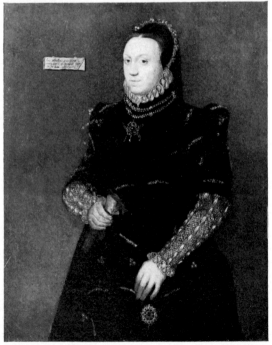

39 (left)

John Lumley, 1st Lord Lumley 1563

The Earl of Scarbrough
Oil on panel 37½ × 31 inches

Documented. Recorded in the Lumley Inventory of 1590: *of your Lordship done by Steven.* This is the first time that the picture has been exhibited since cleaning and restoration.

John, Lord Lumley (1534 ?–1609) was implicated in the Catholic intrigues against Elizabeth and was sent to the Tower 1569. Although he later regained his reputation, his position as a catholic kept him out of public life and he lived increasingly as a recluse, surrounded by the treasures of Lumley Castle. (See no. 92).

40 (bottom left)

Jane FitzAlan, Lady Lumley 1563

The Earl of Scarbrough
Oil on panel, 37½ × 31 inches

Companion portrait to no. 39. Jane FitzAlan (153 ?–1576/7) was daughter of the last Earl of Arundel and sister of Mary, Duchess of Norfolk (no. 30). Through her the Arundel collection came to Lord Lumley which probably included the Holbein cartoon of Henry VIII (now in the National Portrait Gallery) and the Holbein drawings (now in the Royal Library at Windsor Castle).

41

Eleanor Bendlowes 1565

St. John's College, Cambridge
Oil on panel, 34 × 27⅞ inches

Attributed. Eleanor Bendlowes was the wife of William Bendlowes (1516–1584), serjeant-at-law, who was educated for a time at St. John's College, Cambridge.

42

Ralph Sheldon 1565

C. Fitzherbert, Esq.
Oil on panel, 33½ × 42½ inches

Attributed. Ralph Sheldon (1537–1613) was son of William Sheldon of Weston. He inherited from his father the Sheldon tapestry works.

An unidentified primitive painter working in the manner of Eworth. A group of pictures, flat and two-dimensional in quality, seem to be the product of a single studio in the sixties. Other instances of his work are *William Brooke, 10th Lord Cobham and his family* (1567 : *Marquess of Bath*) and *Edward, 3rd Lord Windsor and his family* (1568 : *Marquess of Bute*). In his predilection for gay pattern and colour he anticipates the high Elizabethan style of the eighties.

43

Frances Sidney, Countess of Sussex *circa* 1565

Sidney Sussex College, Cambridge
Oil on panel, 76 × 43¾ inches

Attributed. Undoubtedly Steven's most spectacular portrait. It was reduced slightly at each side at a later date which accounts for the otherwise somewhat odd shape.

Frances Sidney, Countess of Sussex (died 1589) was sister of Sir Henry Sidney and Sir Philip's aunt. She married Sussex in 1555 and on her death left £5,000 for erecting a college in the University of Cambridge to be called 'Lady Frances Sidney College'.

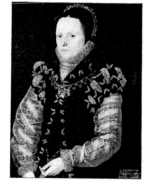

44

Anne Russell, Countess of Warwick *circa* 1565

The Duke of Bedford and the Trustees of the Bedford Settled Estates
Oil on panel, 21 × 16½ inches

Attributed. Anne Russell (1548–1604) was daughter of the 2nd Earl of Bedford. She married Ambrose Dudley, Earl of Warwick in 1565. Lady Anne Clifford records in her *Diary* that the Countess 'came to serve Queen Elizabeth when she was very young; so as she served that illustrious Queen, when she was maid, wife and widdow . . . till the said Queen's death, and she was more beloved and in greater favour with the said Queen than any other lady or woman in the kingdom'.

45

Katherine de Vere, Lady Windsor 1567

David Arkwright, Esq.
Oil on panel, 18½ × 13¾ inches

Attributed. Exhibited after cleaning and restoration. The same figure occurs in the group portrait of her, her husband and children painted the same year (*Marquess of Bute coll.*). Katherine de Vere (died 1600) was eldest daughter of the 16th Earl of Oxford. She married Windsor *circa* 1553–58.

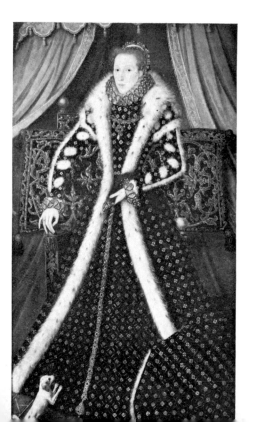

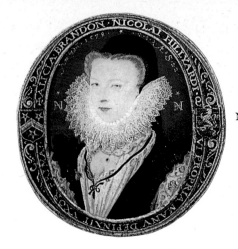

Nicholas Hilliard *Alice Hilliard* (no. 82)

46

Mary Hill, Mrs Mackwilliam 1567

The Lord Tollemache
Oil on panel, 33 × 24 inches

Attributed. Mary Hill was daughter of Richard Hill, Sergeant of the Cellar to Henry VIII. Henry Mackwilliam was her second husband. Her grand-daughter married the 2nd Baronet.

47

Unknown Lady 1567

The Lord Tollemache
Oil on panel, 26¾ × 21 inches

Attributed. Possibly Dorothy Wentworth, Mrs Tollemache. She was the daughter of Sir Richard Wentworth of Nettlestead and wife of the second Lionel Tollemache of Helmingham.

48 (right)

Unknown Girl 1569

The Tate Gallery
Oil on panel, 24¾ × 19 inches

Attributed.

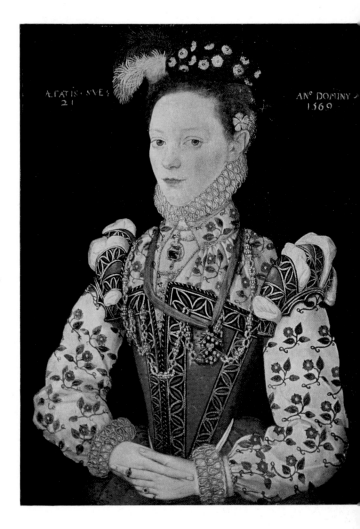

ARNOLD VAN BROUNCKHORST flourished 1565/6–1580

Flemish painter of mediocre talent who eventually became court painter to James VI of Scotland. He purveyed a feeble style based on that evolved by Antonio Mor. Brounkhorst may well turn out to be responsible for the endless mechanical images of Elizabethan court officials that start to be produced in number in the late sixties.

49

William Cecil, Lord Burghley 1573

The Marquess of Salisbury
Oil on panel, $37\frac{1}{4} \times 28$ inches

Signed on the column left: *A 1573 B*. The portrait is a version of an earlier one at Hatfield, updated by the insertion of the Lord Treasurer's wand of office.

William Cecil, Lord Burghley (1520–1598) was Elizabeth's first minister, a man of outstanding genius and immense industry. He had a taste for architecture and gardens and built three great houses.

50

James VI of Scotland 1574

The Scottish National Portrait Gallery
Oil on panel, 17×11 inches

Attributed. Fragment of a full length portrait, the appearance of which is known through later copies that preserve the 1574 date (e.g. National Portrait Gallery, London). (See no. 174).

51

James Douglas, 4th Earl of Morton *circa* 1575

The Scottish National Portrait Gallery
Oil on panel, $41\frac{3}{4} \times 32$ inches

Attributed. James, Earl of Morton (died 1581), leading Protestant Scottish nobleman, who led the conspiracy to murder Mary Queen of Scots favourite, Rizzio. Generally followed an opportunist policy and was eventually, 1572, Regent for James VI. Ousted by Argyll and Atholl from the Regency, 1578, and eventually executed for the murder of Darnley.

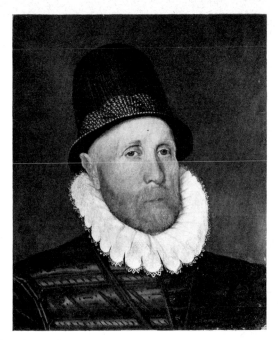

52 (above)

Oliver St. John, 1st Baron St. John of Bletso 1578

The Hon. Hugh Lawson-Johnston
Oil on panel, $18\frac{1}{2} \times 15\frac{1}{2}$ inches

Signed along the left edge of the panel: *AR BRONCK-HORST FECIT* 1578. Lord St. John (died 1582) was one of the peers who sat on the trial of the Duke of Norfolk.

CORNELIUS KETEL flourished 1548–1616

Painter of Gouda who worked in England 1573–81. He was introduced to Sir Christopher Hatten and Elizabeth sat to him in 1578. His style is close to the robust bourgeois tradition of William Key.

53

William Gresham 1579

Private Collection
Oil on panel, $40\frac{1}{2} \times 30\frac{1}{2}$ inches

Signed. William Gresham of Titsey (1522–1579) was the son of Sir John Gresham of Holt, the founder of the Russia Company. He was sheriff of Surrey and Sussex from 1564 to 1577.

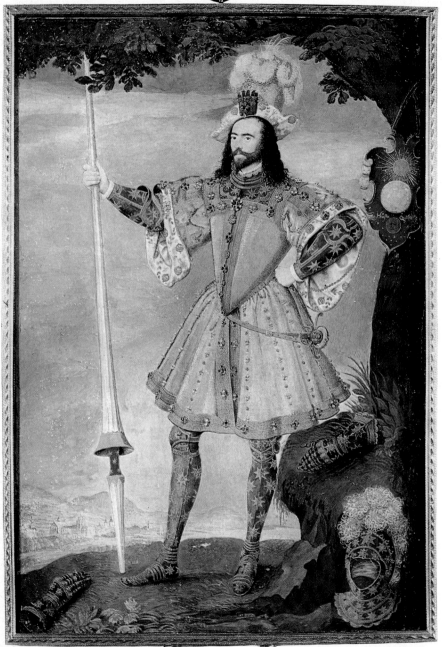

Elizabethan

Nicholas Hilliard
George Clifford, 3rd Earl of Cumberland
(no. 56)

III

and Jacobean Chivalry

Lo, they sound; the knights, in order armed,
Ent'ring thereat the list, addressed to combat
For their courtly loves; he, he's the wonder
      Whom Eliza graceth.
Their plumed pomp the vulgar heaps detaineth,
And rough steeds: let us the still devices
Close observe, the speeches and the musics
      Peaceful arms adorning.

POEM ON AN ACCESSION DAY TILT BY THOMAS CAMPION

A CHRONICLE OF EVENTS 1570–1603

1572	The Ridolfi Plot. **Hilliard's first known miniature of Elizabeth I** (no. 72). Peace with France: Eworth designs costumes and décor for the fêtes to welcome the French commissioners.
1575	Leicester entertains Elizabeth at Kenilworth. Sir Henry Lee entertains Elizabeth at Woodstock. **Federigo Zuccaro visits England** (nos. 74 and 91).
1576–78	**Hilliard in France.**
1579	Spenser's *Shepheardes Calendar* published. The match between Elizabeth and the Duke of Anjou at its height.
1583	The Throckmorton Plot.
1585	England openly intervenes in the Low Countries. War with Spain.
1586	The Babington Plot.
1587	Execution of Mary Queen of Scots. Drake raids Cadiz.
1588	Defeat of the Spanish Armada. **Gower paints Elizabeth I** (no. 76).
1589	Spenser's *Faerie Queene* published.
1590	Cumberland succeeds Sir Henry Lee as Queen's Champion (no. 56).
1592	Sir Henry Lee entertains Elizabeth at Ditchley. **Gheeraerts paints the Ditchley portrait** (no. 78).
1596	The Cadiz Expedition. **Gheeraerts paints Essex** (no. 157).
1601	Essex rebellion.
1603	Death of Elizabeth I.

The Cult of Chivalry

The culture of the Elizabethan court was fundamentally a chivalrous one. Although the political and social obligations of chivalry had long since vanished, its etiquette and mythology were revitalised and chivalry was now overlaid with a fashionable neoplatonic gloss. The cult of the Queen hinged on her dual role both as the sovereign claiming the loyalty of her knights and as the adored, idealised, lady in whose honour knights fought at the tilt. The great spectacles and entertainments of the age were tilts, tournaments and barriers; its great publications were romances of chivalry, and its architecture drew directly for its inspiration on late Gothic churches and castles. Even as late as 1610 Prince Henry, James I's eldest son, was still being framed by Ben Jonson with imagery of Arthurian romance.

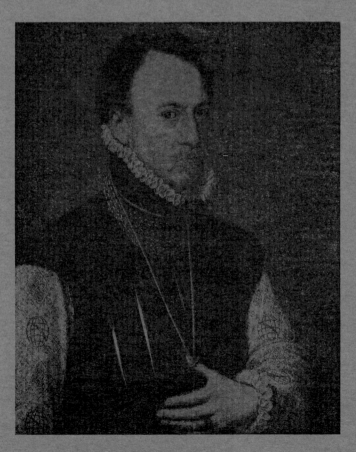

54
ANTONIO MOR
Sir Henry Lee 1568

The National Portrait Gallery
Oil on panel, 25¼ × 21 inches

Sir Henry Lee (1533–1611) occupies a central role in the creation of the mythology of the Elizabethan court. He had a highly successful career and was Elizabeth's Master of The Armoury. Camden states that at the beginning of the reign he issued a challenge to run a tilt against all comers annually on the Queen's Accession Day, November 17th. From this vow arose a series of tournaments which, by the early eighties, had reached spectacular proportions. Under Lee's auspices there was even a continuity of imagery sustained. To these festivals knights came in elaborate fancy dress surrounded by actors and musicians who acted out dramas in the tilt yard. Lee gave Elizabeth two famous entertainments on progress, one at Woodstock in 1575, in which the Fairy Queen made her first appearance, and one in 1592 at Ditchley, two years after his retirement as champion, in which he recalled to Elizabeth all he had done in creating her legend (see no. 78). He sat for Mor while in the Low Countries in 1568; was a notable patron of Gheeraerts and probably compiled the programme for the Ditchley Portrait. (no. 78).

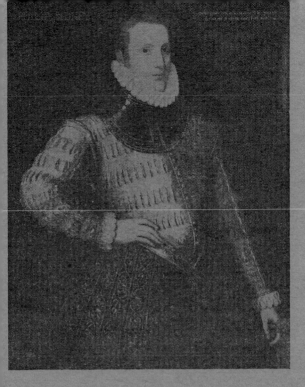

55 (above)
ARTIST UNKNOWN

Sir Philip Sidney

The Marquess of Bath
Oil on panel, 45 × 33 inches

Sidney (1554–1588) epitomised the Elizabethan chivalrous ideal. An astute politician who worked relentlessly, often in the face of the Queen, for a European pan-Protestant league, he was also a cultivated renaissance man of letters. No other work shows quite so clearly the impact of the chivalry cult at court during the eighties than his *Arcadia* (no. 67). Sidney's death as a result of a wound at the battle of Zutphen signalled the creation of a national hero.

One of three versions of this portrait showing Sidney at the age of twenty-three.

56
NICHOLAS HILLIARD *circa* 1590

George Clifford, 3rd Earl of Cumberland

National Maritime Museum, Greenwich
Miniature, $10\frac{1}{8}$ × 7 inches
Illustrated in colour on page 32

Cumberland succeeded Sir Henry Lee (no. 54) as Queen's Champion at the Tilt on November 17th 1590. From that year onwards Clifford headed the challengers at each year's Accession Day Tilt in his disguise as Knight of Pendragon Castle. In 1590, when he succeeded, he arrived on a castle surrounded by figures from Arthurian romance. In 1595 he came on 'a dragon, laiden with fair spoils'. Hilliard depicts him in this chivalrous role (there is a castle in the distance to the left). He is shown in the act of challenging with his gauntlet flung down and he wears an elaborate allegorical costume: star-studded armour, a surcoat embroidered with caducei, branches of olive and celestial spheres (see also nos. 54 and 78) and the Queen's glove is pinned to the front of his bonnet. Astrological imagery was very popular with tilters.

On the tree to the right hangs a little pasteboard shield on which there is the knight's *impresa*. These shields were also presented in court masques and the type of costume which knights jousted in before the Queen must have been forerunners of Inigo Jones's masque costume in the new century (see no. 176).

George, 3rd Earl of Cumberland (1558–1605) was a naval commander who led expeditions, mostly unsuccessfully, against the Spaniards.

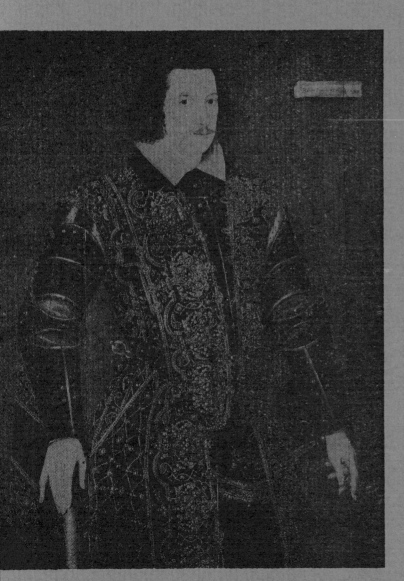

57
WILLIAM SEGAR

Robert Devereux, 2nd Earl of Essex

National Gallery of Ireland, Dublin
Oil on panel, 44½ × 34½ inches

Documented. Recorded among the six portraits by Segar in the Lumley Inventory of 1590: *of the second Earle of Essex (Robert) Devereux, Master of the Horse done by Seigar.* The portrait was probably once a full length as two 18th-century sources describe it as such. Essex is shown here before he grew a beard and probably in the fancy dress he wore at the Accession Day Tilt of 1590:

> . . . all in Sable sad,
> Drawen on with cole-black Steeds of duskie hue,
> In stately Chariot full of deepe device . . .
>
> (GEORGE PEEL Polyhymnia)

Essex's sensational entrance at the Tilt disguised as a funeral cortège was to implore the Queen's pardon for his marriage to Sidney's widow, Frances Walsingham. During the nineties Essex played a leading role in the spectacular fêtes which marked Elizabeth's Accession Day. Francis Bacon was employed to write elaborate speeches to frame Essex's appearances. Through Essex and Cumberland Elizabethan chivalry reached its height in the post-Armada years.

Robert Devereux, 2nd Earl of Essex (1566–1601) was Elizabeth's last favourite and her Master of the Horse. He led military expeditions to France, Cadiz and Ireland but the circle that centred on him lost its bid for power in the struggle with Robert Cecil. A desperate rebellion, when he and his friends tried to raise London and seize the Queen, ended in disaster and his execution.

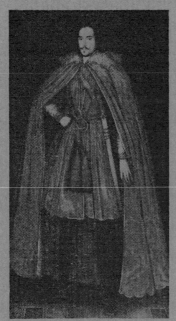

58

Attributed to ROBERT PEAKE

Edward Herbert, Lord Herbert of Cherbury *circa* 1604

The National Trust, Powis Castle
Oil on canvas, 85 × 45 inches

In 1604 the ceremonies for creation of Knights of the Bath
were enacted for the first time for half a century at the
coronation of James I. These medieval rites were performed in
full detail, as narrated by the sitter, the first day wearing the
gown of a religious order, then the bath, 'the second day to
wear robes of crimson taffety (in which habit I am painted in
my study,) . . . and the third day to wear a gown of purple silk,
upon the left sleeve whereof is fastened certain strings weaved
of white silk and gold tied in a knot, and labels to it of the same,
which all the knights are obliged to wear until they have done
something famous in arms, or until some lady of honour take it
off, and fasten it on her sleeve . . . I had not worn long this
string, but a principal lady of the court, and, certainly in men's
opinion, the handsomest, took mine off, and said she would
pledge her honour for mine.'

Lord Herbert of Cherbury (1583–1648), philosopher and
diplomatist, was ambassador to Paris 1619–24. He wrote a
famous autobiography, a *Life of Henry VIII* and a philosophical
treatise, *De Veritate*.

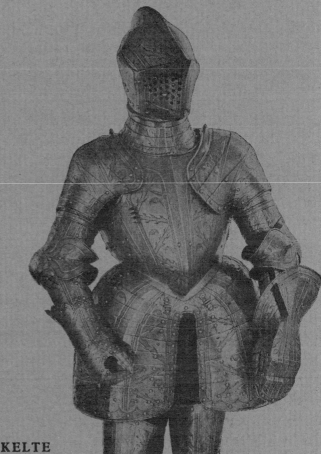

59

JOHN KELTE

Armour of Robert Dudley, Earl of Leicester *circa* 1565

Her Majesty's Armouries, Tower of London
height, 70 inches

A splendid Greenwich armour made for Robert Dudley, Earl
of Leicester (see no. 91). It is described in an inventory of 1611
as 'one Tylte armour compleate graven with the pegged staffe
made for the Earle of Leicester'. Leicester tilted a great deal in
the sixties and even as late as 1582 made an appearance at the
great *Barriers* for Anjou at Whitehall, when the French Duke
entered on a rock drawn by golden chains held by Love and
Destiny.

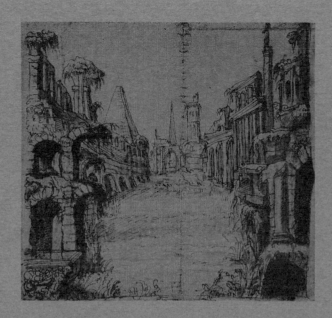

INIGO JONES

DESIGNS FOR BEN JONSON'S *BARRIERS* 1610

60

The Fallen House of Chivalry

The Trustees of the Chatsworth Settlement
Drawing, $9\frac{1}{2} \times 10\frac{1}{2}$ inches
See no. 61.

61

St. George's Portico

The Trustees of the Chatsworth Settlement
Drawing, $10\frac{3}{8} \times 12\frac{1}{4}$ inches

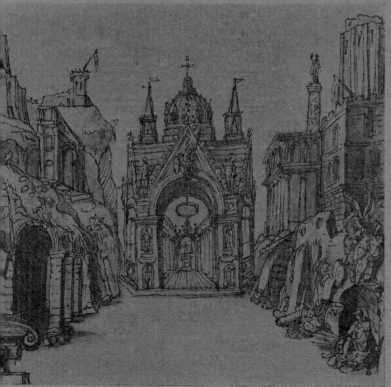

Designs by Inigo Jones for the *Barriers* of 1610. The latter
were occasioned by Prince Henry's first appearance in arms for
which he took the pseudonym, Meliadus, Lord of the Isles.
The Prince and his six companions issued a challenge on
December 31st and the Barriers were performed in the Whitehall Banqueting House on Twelfth Night. In Prince Henry
mingled the dual streams of a new baroque prince (see
Epilogue) and a revival of chivalry within the Elizabethan
tradition. Ben Jonson's script for the Barriers casts the Prince
in the role of the reviver of Chivalry whose house now lay
'Flat with the earth'. King Arthur appears and presents Prince
Henry with a shield and Henry and his assistants are
'discovered' sitting in St. George's Portico 'yet undemolished'.
This is the central building in the drawing, while to the right
Chivalry in her cave waits to emerge to hail the Prince as her
deliverer:

> . . . Break, you rusty doors,
> That have so long been shut, and from all shores
> of all the world come knighthood, like a flood
> Upon these lists. . . .

Inigo is still thinking in Gothic terms and the scene is full of
Norman and Gothic arches and battlements.

ELIZABETHAN NEO-GOTHIC ARCHITECTURE

Elizabethan architects, particularly in the late eighties and nineties, were inspired more by late Gothic than the new classicism. This was the hey-day of neo-medievalism which produced a crop of houses with acres of glass (*e.g.* Hardwick), and romantic castles, culminating in Bolsover. The theme of Elizabethan chivalry thus finds concrete expression in the architecture of the era. These five drawings show such neo-medieval buildings.

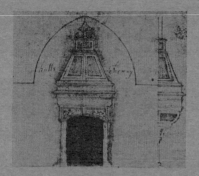

62

ROBERT SMYTHSON died 1614

Design for the Front of an Unidentified House 1580–90

Drawings Collection, Royal Institute of British Architects
Drawing, 13 × 18 inches

Possibly a first design for Hardwick, one of Smythson's most important projects.

63

JOHN SMYTHSON died 1634

Design for the Vaulted Room in the Keep, Bolsover Castle, Derbyshire 1612–16

Drawings Collection, Royal Institute of British Architects
Drawing, 9 × 4¾ inches
See no. 64.

64 (left)

Design for the Chimney Piece in the Hall, Bolsover Castle, Derbyshire 1612–16

Drawings Collection, Royal Institute of British Architects
Drawing, 4½ × 5 inches

Sir Charles Cavendish began building at Bolsover in 1612. His house epitomises the spirit of Jacobean chivalry and romance. The Serlian Hall chimney piece is dated 1616.

no. 65

65

Design for Slingsby Castle, North Riding, Yorkshire circa 1620–30

Drawings Collection, Royal Institute of British Architects
Drawing, 6 × 9 inches
See no. 66.

66

Design for Slingsby Castle, North Riding, Yorkshire circa 1620–30

Drawings Collection, Royal Institute of British Architects
Drawing, 5 × 8¼ inches

Slingsby was probably built in the 1620's by Sir Charles Cavendish, brother of William Cavendish, Duke of Newcastle, for whom John Smythson was then working at Welbeck Abbey. Like Bolsover, it evokes knightly associations. Sir Charles Cavendish, although a dwarf, was a gallant soldier, a philosopher, a correspondent of Descartes and Gassendi, and a man with 'a lovely and beautiful soul'.

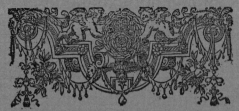

HONOR
Military, and Ciuill, contained in foure Bookes.
Viz.

1. Juſtice, and Iuriſdiction Military.
2. Knighthood in generall, and particular.
3. Combats for life, and Triumph.
4. Precedencie of great Eſtates, and others.

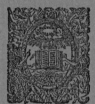

¶IMPRINTED AT LON-
don by *Robert Barker*, Printer to the
Queenes moſt Excellent
Maieſtie.
ANNO DOM. 1602.

67

SIR PHILIP SIDNEY

The Countess of Pembroke's Arcadia 1590

The British Museum Library

An important instance of the influence of Elizabethan chivalry.
Written originally by Sidney in imitation of classical Greek
romance, he recast it in the eighties, inserting long descriptions
of chivalrous combats. The book is open at a passage where he
is alluding to an actual Elizabethan tilt in which Laelius
(Sir Henry Lee), who comes chained with a nymph leading
him, tilts against Philisides (Sidney), dressed as a shepherd
knight with a train of servants playing bagpipes and his lances
disguised as sheep hooks.

68

EDMUND SPENSER

The Faerie Queene 1590

The British Museum Library

The first three books of the Faerie Queene, the quintessence of
the whole Gloriana cult in which Protestant theology,
renaissance cosmology, Elizabethan chivalry and visions of the
Imperial Virgin, Elizabeth, are woven into a single tapestry.
No other book reflects so admirably the thought context of the
age in which apparently dissimilar ideas are part of a
coherent pattern.

69

ARIOSTO

Orlando Furioso
translated by SIR JOHN HARINGTON 1591

The British Museum Library

An instance of the Elizabethan passion for romance,
Harrington's translation of Ariosto's great chivalrous epic. It is
illustrated with engravings in perspective which, Harrington
explains, causes things near to be large and far away small.

70

WILLIAM SEGAR

Honor Military and Civill 1602

The British Museum Library

On Segar, herald and painter, see nos. 57, 124–7.

An amplified version of William Segar's *Book of Honor and
Armes* (1589) it contains engravings by William Rogers,
probably after drawings by Segar, of knights in the habits of
various orders of chivalry. The book gives the fullest surviving
account of Elizabethan chivalrous exercises and includes an
interesting chapter on monuments and epitaphs. Here Segar
provides the context of Elizabethan portraiture quoting
Scipio's belief that 'Portratures, Pictures, and other
Monuments were devised to ornifie Temples, Cities, and
Princes pallaces . . . to retaine in memory, the excellent
Actions of such men, as had lived honourably, and died
vertuously.'

IV

Gloriana

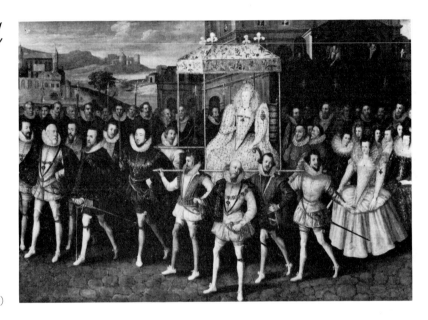

Attributed to Robert Peake *Elizabeth I* (no. 80)

Are you then travelling to the temple of Eliza?

Even to her temple are my feeble limbs travelling.
Some call her Pandora: some Gloriana: some
Cynthia: some Belphoebe: some Astraea; all by
several names to express several loves: Yet
all those names make but one celestial body,
as all those loves meet to create but one soul.

I am of her own country, and we adore her by
the name of Eliza.   THOMAS DEKKER *Old Fortunatus*

Portraits of Elizabeth I

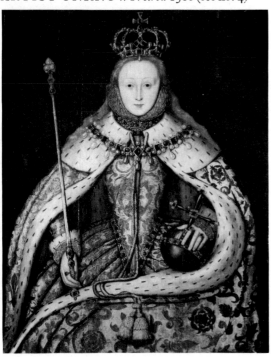

71 (below)
ARTIST UNKNOWN *circa* 1559

The Trustees of the Warwick Castle Resettlement
Panel, 48 × 39 inches

Elizabeth is recorded here as she appeared at her coronation on January 15th 1559: 'one mantle of clothe of golde, tissued with golde and silver, furred with powdered armyons [ermines], with a mantle lace of silke and golde, with buttons and tassells to the same'; 'One kirtle of the same tissue, the traine and skirts furred with powdered armyons, the rest lined with sarce-onet, with a paire of bodies and sleeves to the same'.

(*Wardrobe Inventory*, 1600).

ARTIST UNKNOWN *circa* 1560 (see no. 4)

72
NICHOLAS HILLIARD 1572

National Portrait Gallery
Miniature, 2 × 1⅞ inches

The earliest portrait miniature by Hilliard of the Queen and presumably the result of the sitting which he records in his *Treatise* written at the close of the reign. This is so important that it must be quoted in full. Elizabeth had asked why the Italians, the best painters, used no shadow in their work. Hilliard replied that shadow was only made use of by painters whose pictures possessed a 'grosser line'. 'Heer', he says, 'her Majestie conseued the reason, and therfore chosse her place to sit in for that purposse in the open ally of a goodly garden, where no tree was neere, nor anye shadowe at all . . .'

This conversation explains much of the aesthetic of high Elizabethan painting in which shadow is totally eliminated.

73
NICHOLAS HILLIARD *circa* 1575

The National Portrait Gallery on loan to the Tate Gallery
Oil on panel, 31 × 24 inches
Illustrated in colour on page 44

One of the two known portraits almost certainly by Hilliard himself. The other is in reverse with different costume (Walker Art Gallery, Liverpool). Elizabeth holds a rose in one hand and at her breast one of her favourite emblems, a pendant phoenix arising from the flames. In the hands of the poets this symbol expands and changes meaning. The phoenix was a unique bird which renewed itself by burning and arising from the ages. For Elizabeth it symbolised above all her virginity and her 'oneness'.

74
FEDERIGO ZUCCARO 1575

The British Museum (Department of Prints and Drawings)
Drawing, $12\frac{1}{8} \times 8\frac{3}{4}$ inches

See no. 90 for a discussion of Zuccaro's visit to England. The drawing is inscribed as being executed in London in May 1575 and is the only known certain likeness of Elizabeth from life. To the right there is an indication of an allegory on the Queen's Virtues : the column of Fortitude and Constancy, the serpent of prudence entwining it, the dog of fidelity and the ermine of purity on top of it.

75
Attributed to JOHN BETTES II *circa 1585–90*

F. H. M. FitzRoy Newdegate, Esq.
Oil on panel, $38 \times 32\frac{1}{2}$ inches

This belongs to a group of five portraits of Elizabeth I all from the same studio, probably that of John Bettes. In these images any attempt at depicting a human being has been abandoned in favour of an icon composed of face and hands, embroidery and lace, chairback and arabesque hangings. These were years when England was openly at war with Spain and the Queen was the subject of a succession of plots, the discovery of each one of which engendered yet further adoration.

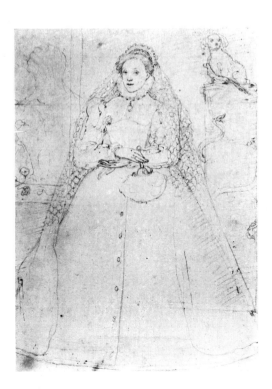

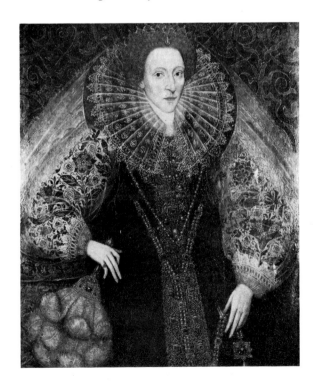

Portraits of Elizabeth I

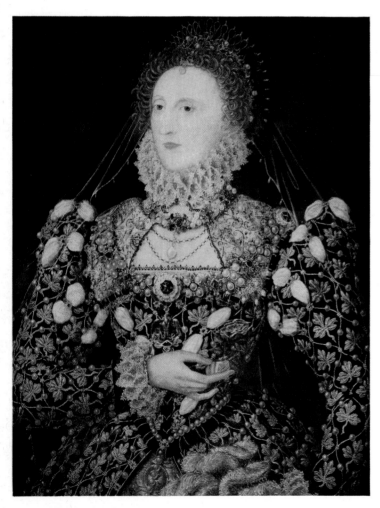

Nicholas Hilliard *Elizabeth I* (no. 73)

76
GEORGE GOWER *circa* 1588

The Duke of Bedford and the Trustees of the Bedford Settled Estates
Oil on panel, $52\frac{1}{2} \times 41\frac{1}{2}$ inches

Painted shortly after the defeat of the Spanish Armada this is a glorification of Elizabeth as 'the worlds Empresse'. This is expressed in the terrestrial globe which her right hand grasps and in the imperial diadem on the table. The theme of prophecies to world empire occur in many other portraits (*e.g.* that in the Pinacoteca di Siena) but reaches a climax after the vanquishing of the might of Spain.

> Still breath our glory, the worlds *Empresse*,
> *Religions* Guardian, *Peaces* patroness!
> Now flourish Arts, the Queene of *Peace* doth raigne;
> Vertue triumph, now she doth sway the stemme,
> Who gives to Vertue honours Diadem.
> (HISTRIO-MASTIX 1589 (?))

To the left the Armada sails towards England while to the right it is wrecked on the rocky coasts of Scotland. The fervour of queen-worship in these years is reflected in the reduction of her image to a formal abstract akin to the principles of a Byzantine Madonna. This is the only portrait of Elizabeth certainly attributable to Gower.

77
NICHOLAS HILLIARD *circa* 1600

Private Collection
Miniature, $2\frac{1}{2} \times 2$ inches

The official image of the Queen in her final years was to be that of an ageless and unfading beauty, the lovely sonnet mistress of successive generations of court poets.

> Times young howres attend her still,
> And her Eyes and Cheekes do fill,
>   With fresh youth and beautie;
> All her louers olde do growe,
> But their hartes, they do not so
>   In their Loue and duty.
> (SIR JOHN DAVIES)

Nicholas Hilliard rejuvenates the features of Elizabeth, then in her middle sixties, back to those of a young girl. This miniature is one of a group of four supposed to have been given by the Queen to Penelope, Lady Rich.

78

MARCUS GHEERAERTS THE YOUNGER 1592?

The National Portrait Gallery
Oil on canvas, 95 × 60 inches
Illustrated in colour as the frontispiece

Inscribed. Together with no. 157 Gheeraerts' masterpiece
from the 1590's, revealing a brilliance in solving the portrayal of
the actuality of the ageing Queen while preserving her myth.
Although the picture has been sadly cut down at both sides
enough remains to capture its spectacular impact. The programme was almost certainly devised by Sir Henry Lee (see
no. 54) for whom it was painted and by long tradition in
connexion with a spectacular entertainment he gave her at his
house at Ditchley in September 1592. On that occasion
Elizabeth made her way through an enchanted wood dispelling
the magic and awakening Lee, discovered in an enchanted
slumber. Lee or Laelius as he styled himself had been
punished for failing, as he had been directed by the Fairy
Queen, to act as the constant custodian of 'enchanted pictures'.
For this offence the Fairy Queen had cast him into a spell-
bound sleep from which Elizabeth now awakes him. It may be
that this portrait was part of the décor on this occasion.

In it Elizabeth arises as a cosmic figure standing on a globe
of the world (her feet on Ditchley). She banishes storms and
ushers in sunshine and the sonnet hails her as surpassing the
sun in brilliance. In her ear is an emblematic ear-ring, an
armillary sphere (see no. 81*xiii*).

79

ISAAC OLIVER

Victoria & Albert Museum
Miniature, $2\frac{3}{8} \times 1\frac{1}{8}$ inches

Unfinished. Closely related to his brother-in-law's realistic
rendering of the Queen (no. 78). Compare this image with
Hilliard's miniatures of her from the same period (no. 77).

80

Attributed to ROBERT PEAKE *circa* 1600

Simon Wingfield Digby, Esq.
Oil on canvas, 52 × 75 inches
Illustrated on page 41

The picture depicts Elizabeth at the close of her reign carried
in procession, an occasion once associated wrongly with the
marriage of Lady Anne Rusell to Lord Herbert at Blackfriars.
Few other images of Elizabeth convey so forcefully the cult
aspect of her being borne as an eternally youthful deity through
town and countryside for the adoration of her subjects.
Monsieur de Maisse, an agent of Henry IV's, gives an account
of the Queen on public progress which answers closely to the
picture:

'When the Queen goes abroad in public the Lord Chamberlain
walks first, being followed by all the nobility who are in court,
and the Knights of the Order (of the Garter) that are present
walk after, near the Queen's person, such as the Earl of Essex,
the Admiral and others. After come the six heralds who bear
maces before the Queen. After her march fifty gentlemen of the
Guard, each carrying a halberd, and sumptuously attired; and
after that the maids and ladies who accompany them very well
attired.'

Here the Gentlemen Pensioners line the route and ahead of the
Queen are, reading from left to right, the following Garter
Knights.

  (i) Edmund Sheffield, 3rd Lord Sheffield and
       1st Earl of Mulgrave.
 (ii) Charles Howard, Lord Howard of Effingham,
       Earl of Nottingham.
(iii) George Clifford, 3rd Earl of Cumberland.
 (iv) Thomas Butler, 10th Earl of Ormonde.
  (v) Unknown.
 (vi) George Talbot, 7th Earl of Shrewsbury.
(vii) Edward Somerset, 4th Earl of Worcester.

The picture has been cut down at the top and sides.

OBELISK designed by Pauline Whitehouse

Elizabeth I surrounded herself with a very coherent and elaborate symbolism which celebrated her in the two roles defined by Spenser both as 'a most royall Queene or Empresse' and as 'a most vertuous and beautiful Lady'. William Camden writing in the reign of James I observed that it would take a whole book to describe the devices she used. On the obelisk are depicted thirteen of her most common symbols and four of her names:

i   The Sieve

The sieve was the attribute of the Vestal Virgin Tuccia who, on being accused of impurity, had seized a sieve and, filling it with water from the Tiber ran without spilling a drop to the Temple of Vesta. It is, therefore, an attribute of chastity and occurs frequently in portraits of the Queen (*e.g.* Pinacoteca di Siena) often combined with a motto which makes it also allude to its sifting action and hence the Queen's discernment. A Vestal Virgin Temple was built for the decor of the 1590 Accession Day Tilt.

ii   Crescent Moon

Cynthia, Diana, or Belphoebe, the moon goddess hymned by Jonson, Chapman, Raleigh and Spenser. References to this role in the portraits take the form of a crescent moon jewel. The moon-cult embraced a wide range from 'Cynthia, queen of seas and lands' to the esoteric allusions of Chapman in which it is linked to 'the forces of the mind'.

iii   The Eglantine

A single white rose emblematic of chastity. Sir Arthur Gorges wrote a long poem glorifying her as the *Eglantine of Merifleur*. Contemporary engravings frame her between the double Tudor Rose and the eglantine.

iv   The Pelican

The Pelican in Piety (*i.e.* feeding its young with its own blood) refers to the Queen as mother of her people and, more particularly, as Governor of the Church of England.

v   The Phoenix

This usually appears with the motto *Semper Eadem*. The Phoenix, which was unique and continued its species by burning itself and arising from the flames, was an emblem of chastity. It is an instance of symbols which stress the uniqueness and one-ness of Elizabeth as the promised Imperial Virgin. (See no. 73).

vi   The Crowned Pillar

The pillar of constancy and fortitude sometimes appears in her portraits (*e.g.* no. 74). A crowned pillar encircled by eglantine formed part of the décor of the 1590 Accession Day Tilt.

vii   The Ermine

The ermine is an emblem of chastity. Rather than soil its pure white fur it would die. The famous 'Ermine Portrait' at Hatfield shows Elizabeth with an ermine nestling on her sleeve. (See no. 74).

viii   The Sword

The Sword of Justice, often with the Bible, was used from the time of Henry VIII onwards with great constancy to refer to the *Justitia* of the kings of England ushering in the Gospel.

ix   The Globe of the World

This appears in portraits sometimes with the motto: *Tutto vedo e molto mancha*. (I see all and much is lacking).

x   The Olive

The attribute of peace. Sometimes Elizabeth actually appears as *Pax* holding a sprig of olive (*e.g.* William Rogers' engraving, *Eliza Triumphans*).

xi   The Rainbow

Symbol of peace after storms. In the famous 'Rainbow Portrait' at Hatfield she holds a rainbow with the motto NON SINE SOLE IRIS (No rainbow without the sun).

xii   Spring Flowers

In the Golden Age spring reigned eternally. Elizabeth ushers in the Golden Age of religious and political purity and calm. Poets and writers usually celebrate her as Astraea, the Virgin of Vergil's *IV Ecologue* whose return brings eternal springtime.

xiii   The Celestial Globe

The meaning of this is obscure. Elizabeth wears a celestial globe ear-ring in the 'Ditchley Portrait' (no. 78). Lee has spheres on his sleeves (no. 54) and Cumberland, his successor as Queen's Champion, also (no. 56).

V

Hilliard and his Contemporaries

> . . . a hand, or eye
> By *Hilliard* drawne, is worth an history,
> By a worse painter made . . .

JOHN DONNE *The Storm*

NICHOLAS HILLIARD 1547–1619

Hilliard is the most important artistic personality of the Elizabethan age. Born in Exeter he was trained by the Queen's goldsmith and emerges in the early seventies as a fully fledged miniaturist under royal and noble patronage. Apart from a brief spell in the employ of the Duke of Anjou (1576–78) Hilliard lived and worked in England as a miniaturist first to Elizabeth I and then to her successor, James I. His style, he writes, was based on Holbein's but he was also influenced particularly by French court portraiture (*e.g.* no. 82). It was a style which found favour with the Queen (see no. 72), one based on line and the use of brilliant colour applied to a shadowless world. His impact on large-scale painting, which he occasionally practised himself (*e.g.* no. 73), was immense. Hilliard trained Segar and Lockey and had a profound influence on Peake, Gower, Larkin and Custodis. In the nineties his style lost favour at court to his pupil Oliver, patronised by the younger generation.

ELIZABETH I, 1572 (see no. 72)
ELIZABETH I, *circa* 1575 (see no. 73)

82
Alice Hilliard 1578

Victoria & Albert Museum
Miniature, 2⅜ inches diameter
Illustrated in colour on page 30

Painted in France where Hilliard was in the service of Francis, Duke of Alençon from 1576 to 1578. This is a particularly good instance of the influence of French art on Hilliard and can be paralleled with chalk portrait drawings by Clouet. Nicholas Hilliard married Alice Brandon in 1576. Alice was the daughter of Robert Brandon, the Queen's goldsmith, to whom Hilliard was apprenticed at the age of fifteen.

83
Unknown Lady

Private Collection
Miniature, 1¾ × 1½ inches
One of a set including nos. 77, 84 and 88

84
Unknown Man *circa* 1585

Private Collection
Miniature, 2 × 1⅝ inches
One of a set of four (see nos. 77, 83 and 88)

85
Unknown Man *circa* 1590

John Bryson, Esq.
Miniature, 2⅛ × 1¾ inches

An excellent example of Hilliard at the height of his powers and a good instance to demonstrate his relationship and influence, for example, on Segar, (*e.g.* no. 124.)

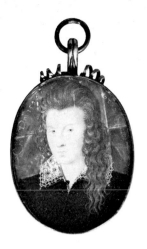

86 (left)

Henry Wriothesley, 3rd Earl of Southampton 1594

The Fitzwilliam Museum, Cambridge
Miniature, $1\frac{5}{8} \times 1\frac{3}{8}$ inches

Southampton (1573–1624) was Shakespeare's patron. Brought up as a royal ward by Lord Burghley he took up his place at court in the nineties in court festivals and as a man of literature. He was an intimate of the Essex circle and took part in the abortive rising of 1601, for which he was imprisoned in the Tower (see no. 173). Although James I showered favours on him, his efforts were confined to colonial endeavours; he was Treasurer of the Virginia Company. He was a great dandy as a young man and wore his hair long and trailing before it became fashionable.

87 (bottom left)

Sir Henry Slingsby 1595

The Fitzwilliam Museum, Cambridge
Miniature, $3\frac{3}{8} \times 2\frac{1}{2}$ inches

In his hat he wears an emblematic jewel, a flower with the motto *SEMPER IDEM*. Sir Henry Slingsby (died 1634) of Scriven, Yorkshire, was father of the royalist of the same name.

88

Unknown Man *circa* 1595

Private Collection
Miniature, $2 \times 1\frac{3}{8}$ inches

One of a set of four (see nos. 77, 83 and 84). This is an excellent instance of the relationship of miniatures to the etiquette of courtly love. The young man is a lover with hand on heart and the miniature was presumably painted for his lady. Elizabethan literature is full of references to miniatures used in this way. In the *Two Noble Kinsmen* Emilia, whose love is sought by the cousins Palamon and Arcite, enters carrying two miniatures:

> Good heaven
> What a sweet face has Arcite?
> . . . and what an eye?
> Of what a frysparkle, and quick sweetnes,
> Has this yong Prince?

ELIZABETH I, *circa* 1600 (see no. 77)

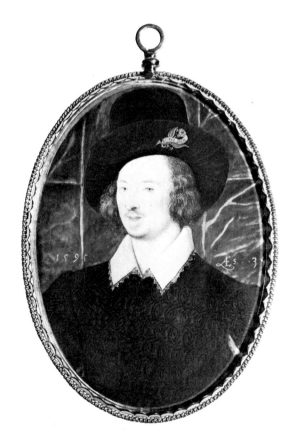

89

A Treatise on the Arte of Limninge

Edinburgh University Library

The only known copy of Hilliard's treatise copied in 1624. This embodies the only aesthetic statement by an artist of the period. Hilliard bases himself extensively on mannerist art theory as purveyed through Haydock's translation of Lomazzo (no. 146) and on various technical treatises. In it he records his encounter with the great of the period — the Queen, Ronsard, Sidney and Hatton.

90 (below)

Letter of the Marchese di Cetona to the Earl of Leicester introducing Federigo Zuccaro March 15th 1575

British Museum (Department of Manuscripts)
Photocopy of Cotton MS.

The letter is to the Earl of Leicester from Chiappino Vitelli, Marchese di Cetona, a general in the Duke of Alva's army in the Netherlands. It is a letter of introduction recommending Zuccaro as one of the most remarkable of Italian painters and as such offers crucial evidence for the length of his visit. Without doubt Zuccaro arrived in England in March 1575 and was back in Italy by October, when he was being canvassed to paint the cupola of Florence Cathedral. During his visit he did two full lengths of the Queen and Leicester (nos. 74 and 91). As the duration of his stay was unknown in the 18th and 19th centuries hundreds of Elizabethan portraits were attributed to him.

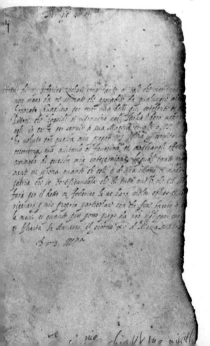

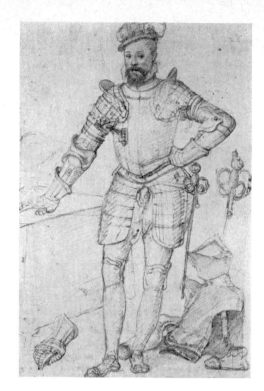

91 (above)

FEDERIGO ZUCCARO 1575
Robert Dudley, Earl of Leicester

The British Museum (Department of Prints and Drawings)
Drawing, $12\frac{3}{4} \times 8$ inches

One of a pair of drawings of Elizabeth and Leicester, designs for full lengths. What was probably the lost Zuccaro of Leicester (but with another armour superimposed over the one in the drawing) was destroyed by enemy action in 1940.

Elizabeth's favourite Leicester occupied an important position as patron of the arts. He patronised Hilliard, he seems to have been instrumental in getting Zuccaro to visit England, and he owned one of the largest portrait collections spread over three houses. Apart from Lord Burghley more portraits of Leicester exist than of any other Elizabethan. This reflects his prime role as a fount of patronage, and his immense vanity. Leicester seems to have sat for his portrait over a dozen times, Lord Burghley thrice.

ELIZABETH I, 1575 (see no. 74).

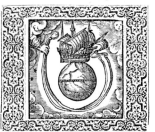

Auxilio diuino. 203

To RICHARD DRAKE *Esquier, in praise of*
Sir FRANCIS DRAKE *Knight.*

THROVGHE scorchinge heate, throughe coulde, in stormes, and
   tempests force,
By ragged rocks, by shelfes,& sandes: this Knighte did keepe his course.
By gapinge gulfes hee pass'd, by monsters of the flood,
By pirattes, theeues, and cruell foes, that long'd to spill his blood.
That wonder greate to scape: but, GOD was on his side,
And throughe them all, in spite of all, his shaken shippe did guide.
And, to requite his paines: By helpe of power deuine.
His happe, at lengthe did aunswere hope, to finde the goulden mine.
Let GRÆCIA then forbeare, to praise her IASON boulde:
Who throughe the watchfull dragons pass'd, to win the fleece of goulde.
Since by MEDEAS helpe, they weare inchaunted all,
And IASON without perrilles, pass'de: the conqueste therfore small?
But, hee, of whome I write, this noble minded DRAKE,
Did bringe away his goulden fleece, when thousand eies did wake.
Wherefore, yee woorthie wightes, that seeke for forreine landes:
Yf that you can, come alwaise home, by GANGES goulden sandes.
And you, that liue at home, and can not brooke the flood,
Geue praise to them, that passe the waues, to doe their countrie good.
Before which sorte, as chiefe: in tempeste, and in calme,
Sir FRANCIS DRAKE, by due deserte, may weare the goulden palme.
     C 2   *Auaritia*

Ouid: Met. lib. 7.

92
INVENTORY OF THE COLLECTION OF JOHN, LORD LUMLEY 1590

The Earl of Scarbrough

Known as the Red Book. This is the most important artistic document of the age as it is the only inventory which occasionally mentions artists' names and, due to Lord Lumley's addition of a painted *cartellino* to his pictures, many are still identifiable. Some are in this exhibition (nos. 34, 36, 38, 39 and 57).

The inventory, which was drawn up in 1590 by John Lampton, Steward of the Household, describes and lists the collection of John, Lord Lumley (see no. 39) at his three residences, Lumley Castle, a house on Tower Hill and Nonsuch Palace, which his father-in-law had purchased from the Crown. It includes a detailed description, including drawings, of the fantastic *mise-èn-scene* Lumley carried out at Lumley Castle. The collection related to this, for not only did Lumley have sets of portraits of his ancestors but went on to surround them with portraits of the monarchs in whose reign he had lived and those of celebrated contemporaries. The criterion was dynastic not aesthetic. James I, on seeing it, remarked 'I didna ken Lumley's ither name was Adam'.

Through his inventory the *oeuvre* of Hans Eworth, Steven van der Muelen, William Segar and Gerlach Flicke have been reconstituted.

93
GEOFFREY WHITNEY

A Choice of Emblemes 1586

The British Museum Library

Whitney's *Choice of Emblemes* is one of the rare English examples of a literary genre which swept Europe in the 16th century. Emblems embodied in visual form a particular moral adage; *imprese* epitomised in image and motto the hopes and aspirations of a particular knight or lady. The medal was one of its most typical forms in which the reverse said in symbolic form the thoughts of the portrait visage on the obverse. Elizabethan portraiture is saturated with emblematics, mostly of an obscure and recondite nature (*e.g.* nos. 57, 121 and 153).

94
FRANCIS MERES

Palladis Tamia, Wits Treasury; being the second part of Wits Commonwealth 1598

The British Museum Library

One of a series of volumes of sententious reflections on morals, religion and literature. In this book, Meres gives an invaluable survey of the arts of his day. The section on painting contains one of the few lists of contemporary English painters.

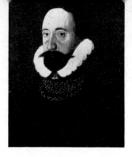

GEORGE GOWER 1540–1596

Throughout the seventies and eighties George Gower was the most fashionable portrait painter in practice. In 1581 he was appointed Sergeant Painter to the Queen and three years later combined with Nicholas Hilliard in an effort to obtain a monopoly over the production of royal portraits. His early work was influenced by French court portraiture, but later he came under the spell of Hilliard and produced a grand series of three-quarters lengths of aristocratic ladies ablaze in gala costume. His work culminates in the great Armada Portrait of Elizabeth I (see no. 76). There are only three certain portraits known by him (nos. 95, 96, 100) but about twenty pictures in all can be reasonably safely attributed to him at this stage.

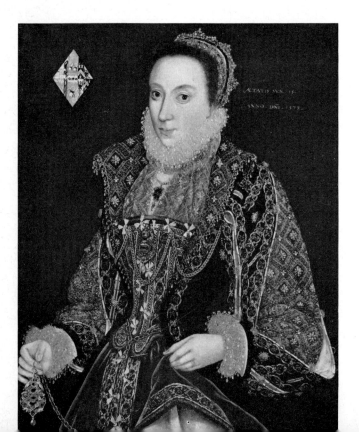

95 (left)
Sir Thomas Kytson 1573

The Tate Gallery
Oil on panel, $20\frac{7}{8} \times 14\frac{7}{8}$ inches

Documented. With no. 96 published by Goodison in 1948 as two out of the five portraits for which payment was made in the 'foreign charges' account for September 1573: *Paid to Gower of London, painter for v pictures v^{li} v^s.* The portrait has been slightly reduced in size at a later date. This and the companion portrait of Lady Kytson are the two pictures upon which all attributions to Gower rest. Many other pictures by Gower were once at Hengrave Hall, the Kytson House in Suffolk, but the collection was dispersed in 1953.

Sir Thomas Kytson (1540–1602) was the son of a wealthy London merchant. He built Hengrave Hall and was a patron of music.

96
Elizabeth Cornwallis, Lady Kytson 1573

The Tate Gallery
Oil on panel, $26\frac{7}{8} \times 20\frac{1}{2}$ inches

Documented. Companion portrait to no. 95. Unlike that of Sir Thomas this has not been reduced in size.

Lady Kytson was daughter of Sir Thomas Cornwallis (see no. 98). Before her marriage she had been one of the household of Margaret, Duchess of Northumberland.

97 (left)
Mary Denton 1573

City of York Art Gallery
Oil on panel, 31×25 inches

Attributed. This picture is more ceremonial than the contemporary portraits of Sir Thomas and Lady Kytson (nos. 95 and 96), but has several features in common, such as the drawing and shape of the head and the way it is set within the ruff collar, the peculiarly sharply drawn eyes, and the cream and pinky buff flesh colours.

Mary Denton was the daughter of Sir Roger Martyn, and married Alexander Denton of Hillesden, Buckinghamshire. It seems highly probable that this is a wedding portrait, which would explain the luxury of the dress and the irregular quartering of the arms of the sitter's husband with those of both her parents.

98

Sir Thomas Cornwallis 1577

The Hon. R. H. C. Neville
Oil on panel, 37 × 28 inches

Attributed. Sir Thomas's daughter was Elizabeth, Lady
Kytson (no. 96). A companion of his wife survives, only in later
copy form, also at Audley End. Sir Thomas Cornwallis
(1519–1614) was Comptroller of the Household to Mary I. A
staunch catholic and loyal servant to Mary, he fell from favour
on Elizabeth's accession and retired to his estates at Brome,
Suffolk.

99

Richard Drake of Esher 1577

National Maritime Museum, Greenwich
Oil on panel, 34½ × 25½ inches

Attributed. Richard Drake (1535–1603) was cousin of Sir
Francis Drake, whose business manager he was. He took charge
of the Spanish prisoners captured off Plymouth in 1588.

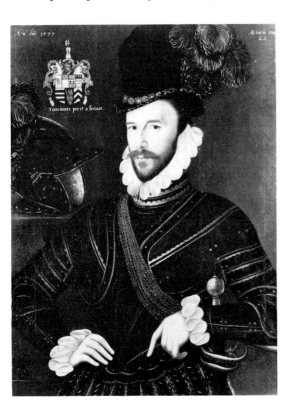

100

George Gower 1579

The Earl Fitzwilliam
Oil on panel, 23¾ × 19½ inches

Signed. This self-portrait is less important as evidence of
Gower's style than for its information on the status of the
painter in Elizabethan England. The verses record his wayward youth during which he was enticed away from 'armes and
vertewe' and his subsequent return to 'pensils trade, wherefore
I must, esteme of it as best'. A Yorkshire gentleman by birth,
he shows the compasses of the painter's craft outweighing his
coat of arms. Later in the reign Nicholas Hilliard, who came of
middle-class stock, argued that he was a gentleman because and
not in spite of his craft.

101

Mary Cornwallis *circa* 1580–85

Manchester City Art Galleries
Oil on panel, 46 × 37 inches

Attributed. Daughter of Sir Thomas Cornwallis (no. 98).

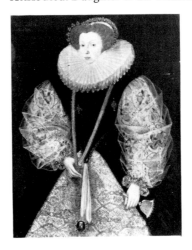

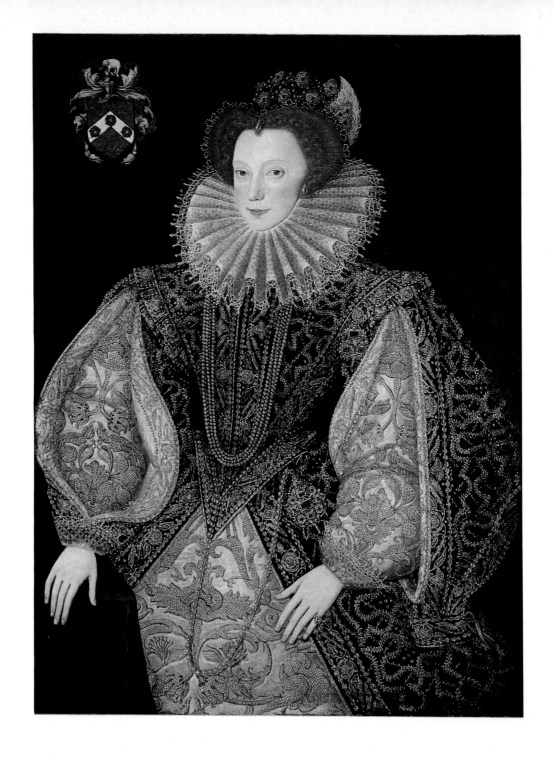

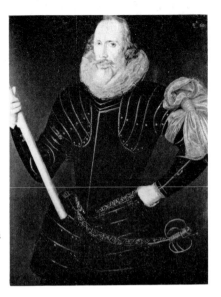

no. 105a

ROBERT PEAKE flourished 1575–1623

Peake was a prolific artist who must have maintained a considerable studio. His *oeuvre* can be very completely reconstructed through one signed picture and a whole series of portraits bearing identical forms of inscribing the date and age of the sitter. (nos. 104, 105, 105a and 107). These early pictures are very much influenced by Hilliard in their handling of the paint and colour range. His work reaches its climax at the turn of the century in ambitious groups, the *Procession of Elizabeth I* (no. 80) and the hunting pieces of Henry, Prince of Wales (no. 110). He became principal painter to Prince Henry, portraits of whom his studio manufactured in great numbers, and later, in 1607, Sergeant Painter to James I jointly with John De Critz. During the Jacobean period he maintained a continuous output of full-length portraits, very variable in quality.

102 (facing page)
Lettice Knollys, Countess of Leicester *circa* 1585

The Marquess of Bath
Oil on canvas, 43 × 32½ inches
Attributed. The portrait was wrongly identified as 'Katherine Parr'. It has the Knollys coat of arms top left and her dress is embroidered with her husband's badge, the ragged staff.

Lettice Knollys (died 1634) was daughter of Sir Francis Knollys. Her first husband was Walter Devereux, Earl of Essex. She was already Leicester's mistress when he married her in 1578, thereby incurring the Queen's lasting displeasure. After Leicester's death in 1588 she married Sir Christopher Blount. She lived to the enormous age of 95 and at 92 she could 'yet walk a mile in the morning'.

103
Elizabeth Sydenham, Lady Drake *circa* 1585

J. B. Gold, Esq.
Oil on canvas, 42 × 32 inches
Attributed. Formerly in the Tyrwhitt-Drake collection at Shardeloes, its identity was suggested by the present owner. Elizabeth Sydenham was Drake's second wife. She was daughter and heiress of Sir George Sydenham and after Drake's death married Sir William Courtney of Powderham.
ELIZABETH I (see no. 76).

104
John Southcote 1589

Private Collection
Oil on panel, 31 × 24½ inches

Inscribed. This is a typical instance of a Peake portrait from the nineties with the form of inscription top left which acts instead of a signature in identifying his work.

105
Sir Thomas Crompton 1590

J. B. Gold, Esq.
Oil on panel, 34½ × 27 inches
Inscribed. Sir Thomas Crompton was a Judge of Admiralty.

105a
Unknown Military Commander 1593

The Lord Rootes
Oil on panel, 44½ × 35¼ inches
Signed on the back of the panel:
M(ADE) BY. ROB(ERT)/PEAKE.
This is the crucial picture which links with certainty the series of portraits which contain an identical way of inscribing the date and age of the sitter to Peake (e.g. nos. 104, 105, 107).
ELIZABETH I, *circa* 1600 (see no. 80).

106

Francis Russell, 4th Earl of Bedford *circa* 1600

The Duke of Bedford and the Trustees of the Bedford Settled Estates
Oil on canvas, 50 × 30½ inches

Attributed. Francis 4th Earl of Bedford (1593–1641) is described by Clarendon as 'a wise man and of too great and plentiful a fortune to wish a subversion of the Government . . . but not incapable, for want of resolution, of being carried into violent courses'.

107

Henry, Prince of Wales 1604

The Earl of Mar and Kellie
Oil on canvas, 53 × 40 inches

Inscribed. (See no. 111). This contains a typical Peake inscription and is the earliest portrait type the artist produced of the Prince.

108 (right)

William Pope, 1st Earl of Downe *circa* 1605

The Viscount Cowdray
Oil on canvas 47 × 85 inches

Attributed. William Pope, 1st Earl of Downe (1573–1631) was created Knight of the Bath, the robes of which he wears in this portrait, at the coronation of James I. At Wroxton Abbey, the Pope house, there was once a remarkable collection of Jacobean portraits now dispersed.

EDWARD, LORD HERBERT OF CHERBURY *circa* 1605

(See no. 59.)

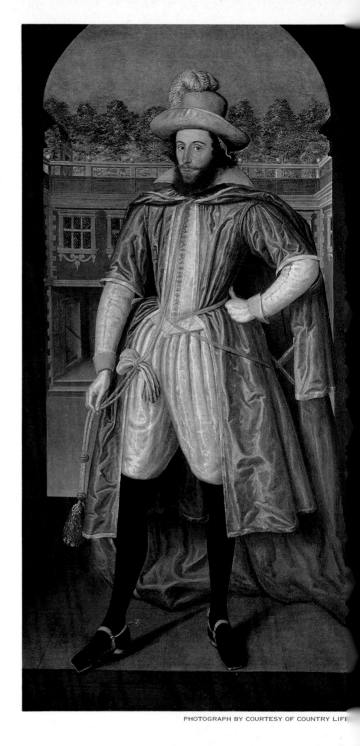

PHOTOGRAPH BY COURTESY OF COUNTRY LIFE

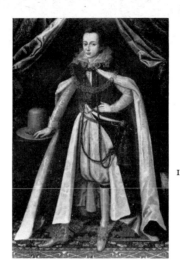
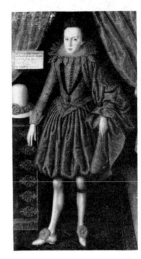

109

Robert Sydney, 1st Earl of Leicester *circa* 1605

The Viscount de L'Isle
Oil on canvas, 79 × 51 inches

Attributed. Presumably identical with the portrait mentioned in the De L'Isle inventory of 1623, 'My Lord Leicester at length in his Viscount robes'. Robert Sydney (1563–1626) was brother to Sir Philip Sydney (see no. 55).

110

Henry, Prince of Wales and Robert Devereux, 3rd Earl of Essex *circa* 1607

Her Majesty The Queen
Oil on canvas, 75 × 65 inches

Attributed. A second version of 1603 bearing typical Peake inscriptions is in the Metropolitan Museum, New York. The earlier picture shows the prince with John, 2nd Lord Harington of Exton.
Robert Devereux (1591–1646) was the son of Elizabeth's favourite (no. 57) and was married at fourteen to Frances Howard (no. 132). They divorced after much scandal in 1613 and she married her lover, Somerset. Over seventeen years later he married Elizabeth Paulet. During the Civil War he went over to Parliament and was General of the Army.

111

Henry, Prince of Wales *circa* 1610

The Marquess of Bath
Oil on canvas, 63 × 33 inches

Attributed. (See no. 107). A typical instance of the numerous full lengths Peake produced of Henry.

112

Charles I as Duke of York *circa* 1610

The Abbot and Community of Ampleforth College
Oil on canvas, 58 × 40 inches

Attributed. Charles was created Duke of York in 1605.

113

Charles I as Prince of Wales *circa* 1612–13

University of Cambridge
Oil on canvas, 62 × 34½ inches

Documented. The portrait commemorates the visit of Charles with his brother-in-law, the Elector Palatine, to the University of Cambridge in March 1612/13. On July 10th Peake was paid £13 6s. 8d. 'in full satisfaction for Prince Charles his picture'.

114

Lady Anne Pope 1615

The Tate Gallery
Oil on panel, 22½ × 17½ inches

Attributed. Recent cleaning has revealed the date 1615, which bears some calligraphic similarity to Peake's known form of inscription.

Lady Anne Pope (died 1629) was the only daughter of Sir William Pope, 1st Earl of Downe. (See no. 108).

JOHN BETTES II flourished 1578/9–1599

A John Bettes is recorded both in 1578/9 and in 1599 as an artist and he has been equated with the management who signed one picture *I.B.* (no. 115). Around this single signed portrait can be grouped a series of hieratic ladies in the Gower manner including probably five portraits of Elizabeth (see no. 75).

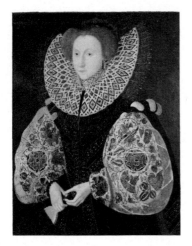

115 (right)
Unknown Girl 1587

St. Olave's and St. Saviour's Grammar School Foundation
Oil on panel, 37 × 30 inches.

Signed. Overpainted to represent Elizabeth I; the signature *I.B.* was discovered in cleaning.

ELIZABETH I, *circa* 1585–90 (see no. 75).

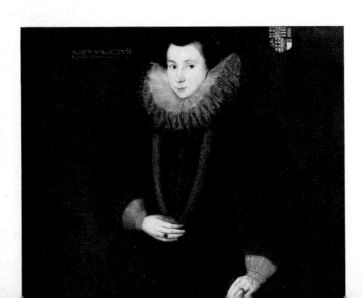

HIERONIMO CUSTODIS flourished 1587–93

Painter from Antwerp whose readily identifiable paintings span a period of six years. Four signed paintings are known and the script on these is repeated on ten others enabling a complete reconstruction of his work in England. While many are of poor quality, particularly in faulty draughtsmanship, he responds at his best to the decorative influence of Hilliard and Gower as in his masterpiece, *Elizabeth, Lady Kennedy* (no. 116).

116
Elizabeth Brydges, later Lady Kennedy 1589

The Duke of Bedford and the Trustees of the Bedford Settled Estates
Oil on panel, $36\frac{1}{4} \times 27\frac{1}{2}$ inches

Signed. Custodis's masterpiece and a picture reflecting the impact of Hilliard on his style. One of two signed pictures by Custodis at Woburn.

Elizabeth Brydges (1575–1617) was one of the two heiress daughters of Lord Chandos. She was 'the fair Mistress Brydges to whom the young Essex showed so much favour as to offend the Queen who 'used words and blows'. She made a disastrous match with Sir John Kennedy (no. 164) in 1603, later fleeing from her husband's house in 'her night gear in fright and starved with cold'. Due to extravagance she died in poverty. Her younger sister Catherine married the 4th Earl of Bedford.

117
Frances Clinton, Lady Chandos 1589

The Duke of Bedford and the Trustees of the Bedford Settled Estates
Oil on canvas transferred from panel, $44\frac{1}{2} \times 34\frac{1}{2}$ inches

Inscribed. Frances Clinton, Lady Chandos (1552–1623) was daughter of Edward Clinton, Earl of Lincoln and Lord High Admiral, and mother of Catherine, Countess of Bedford. Lady Chandos died at Woburn.

118 (left)
Thomasine Browne 1590

Trustees of the Will of J. H. C. Evelyn, deceased
Oil on panel, $35 \times 30\frac{3}{8}$ inches

Inscribed. The portrait has been extended either side at a later date.

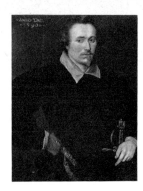

119 (right)

Edward Sheldon 1590

Major C. Fellowes
Oil on panel, 30 × 24 inches

Inscribed. One of a set of three portraits of members of the Sheldon family of Weston painted by Custodis in 1590 (See also no. 120). Edward Sheldon was younger brother of Ralph (See no. 120).

120

Ralph Sheldon 1590

C. Fitzherbert, Esq.
Oil on panel, 31 × 25 inches

Inscribed. (See no 119). Ralph Sheldon (1537–1613) married Anne, daughter of Sir Robert Throckmorton of Coughton Court. A portrait now at Coughton by Custodis, also of 1590, is identified as Anne, Lady Throckmorton. It seems likely that this is in fact a companion portrait to Ralph Sheldon and in fact depicts Anne Throckmorton, Mrs Sheldon.

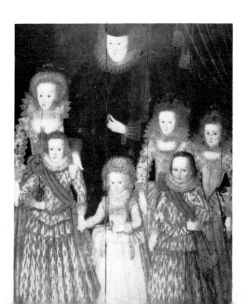

UNKNOWN FOLLOWER OF CUSTODIS
flourished 1593–1612

Primitive painter, probably trained by Custodis and patronised by provincial gentry and bourgeoisie. Further portraits have come to light since the group published in *The English Icon* (1969).

121

Henry Howard Earl of Northampton 1594

The Mercers' Company
Oil on panel, 29½ × 26 inches

Inscribed. Notice the complex emblems of the flower in the snowstorm and the celestial sphere in the sitter's hand.

Northampton (1540–1614) rose to favour under James I being created Earl in 1604 and Lord Privy Seal 1608. He was a Catholic and a man of immense learning. Weldon describes him as 'a great Clerk, yet not a wise man, but the grossest Flatterer of the World' and of 'a venomous and crankred disposition'.

121a

Young girl

Private Collection
Oil on panel, 32 × 23¼ inches

122

Nicholas Wadham *circa* 1595

The Viscountess Galway
Oil on panel, 36 × 28½ inches

Nicholas Wadham (1532–1609) was the founder of Wadham College, Oxford.

123 (left)
ARTIST UNKNOWN

The Tasburgh Group *circa* 1605

Private collection
Oil on panel, 70 × 54 inches

A splendid instance of the genealogical family tree portrait. It shows Lettice Cressy, Lady Tasburgh of Bodney, Norfolk and her children: Dorothy, Penelope, Mary, Lettice, Elizabeth and Katherine. The painter is a provincial one working in the Hilliard manner.

SIR WILLIAM SEGAR died 1633

William Segar was a herald. He began as Portcullis Pursuivant in 1585 and ended as Garter King of Arms in 1603. Fourteen years later James I knighted him. Segar is an extremely difficult artist to disentangle as we only have one documented picture (no. 57). It is unlikely that he continued to paint after 1603 when he became Garter and that his main period of activity was the last two decades of Elizabeth's reign. About a dozen can be tentatively associated with him. His style belongs entirely to the orbit of Nicholas Hilliard and, if the attribution is accepted, his masterpiece is the 'Ermine Portrait' of Elizabeth I at Hatfield House (1585: Marquess of Salisbury).

ROBERT DEVEREUX, 2ND EARL OF ESSEX *circa* 1590 (see no. 57.)

124 (right)
Robert Devereux, 2nd Earl of Essex *circa* 1590

The Earl of Jersey
Oil on panel (oval top), 32¾ × 22 inches
Attributed. (See no. 57).

125
Unknown Man called Sir Walter Raleigh *circa* 1590

Mrs P. Maxwell-Scott
Oil on panel, 43 × 41 inches
Attributed.

126
Eleanor Palmer *circa* 1590

Mrs P. A. Tritton
Oil on panel, 36 × 30 inches
Attributed.

127 (right)
Unknown Lady *circa* 1595–1600

Major General Sir George Burns
Oil on panel, 36½ × 30 inches
Attributed.

WILLIAM LARKIN *flourished circa* 1610–20

William Larkin is one of the great discoveries in English painting if the construction of his *oeuvre* is acceptable. In his pictures the high Elizabethan style evolved by Nicholas Hilliard had one final blaze of glory before going into total eclipse. Little is known of him apart from payments in accounts and references in the diary of Lady Anne Clifford. His *oeuvre* can be pieced together through the use of identical carpets and curtains in whole sets of pictures. Due to their fragile condition the two documented works by him of Lord Herbert of Cherbury and Sir Thomas Lucy at Charlecote could not be included in the exhibition. The series of full lengths from Redlynch (nos. 133–9) are Larkin's masterpieces.

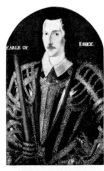

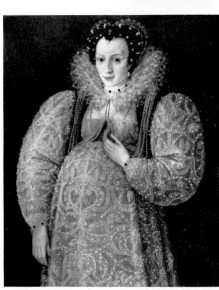

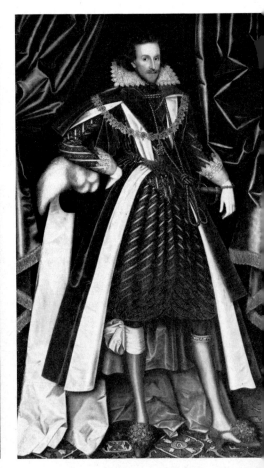

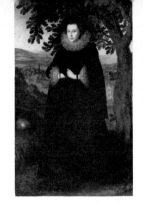

128

Edward Sackville, 4th Earl of Dorset 1613

The Executors of the Estate of the late Countess of Suffolk and Berkshire
Oil on canvas, 80 × 47 inches *Illustrated in colour on page* 62
Attributed. Companion to no. 129 and presumably the same date.

Edward Sackville (1590–1652) succeeded his brother as Earl in 1624. He was Chamberlain to Henrietta Maria and later Chamberlain of the Household. Dorset attended Charles I at Oxford. Clarendon describes him: 'his person [was] beautiful and graceful and vigorous, his wit pleasant, sparkling, and sublime, and his other parts of learning of that lustre that he could not miscarry the vices he had were of the age, which he was not stubborn enough to condemn or resist'.

129

Richard Sackville, 3rd Earl of Dorset 1613

The Executors of the Estate of the late Countess of Suffolk and Berkshire
Oil on canvas, 80 × 47 inches

Attributed. Companion to no. 128 and slightly earlier in date than the seven ladies in the same collection (nos. 133–39).

Dorset (1589–1624), 'a man of spirit and talent, but a licentious spendthrift'. In 1609 he married Anne Clifford, the only daughter and heir of the third Earl of Cumberland (see no. 56).

130 (left)

Philip Herbert, 4th Earl of Pembroke *circa* 1615

The Hon. R. H. C. Neville
Oil on canvas, 84 × 49½ inches

Attributed. Philip Herbert (1584–1650) succeeded his brother in 1630; later he became a parliamentarian. Clarendon says that 'he pretended to no other qualification than to understand dogs and horses'. Patron of Van Dyck. Married Anne Clifford after the death of her first husband, Richard Sackville (see no. 129).

131 (right)

Lady St. John of Bletso *circa* 1615

John Eyston, Esq.
Oil on canvas, 80½ × 48½ inches

Attributed. The identity of the sitter presents problems. She could be Elizabeth Paulet (died 1655) who married (1602) Oliver St. John, 3rd Baron St. John of Bletso and (1624) 1st Earl of Bolingbroke. In the background is one of the earliest landscapes in English painting.

131a

Richard Sackville, 3rd Earl of Dorset *circa* 1615

Lord Sackville
Oil on canvas, 80 × 46 inches
Attributed. (See no. 129). Dorset is a recorded patron Larkin.

132

Frances Howard, Countess of Somerset *circa* 1615–20

The National Portrait Gallery
Oil on panel, 22⅝ × 17¼ inches

Possibly documented. One of the three versions of this portrait, one of which may be her sister, Catherine. The Verney papers at Claydon contain a reference to *Lady Somerset on board by Larkin*. The complications over identity are discussed in R. Strong, *Tudor and Jacobean Portraits*, 1969, I, p. 297

Frances Howard (1590–1632), a notorious beauty, was daughter of Thomas Howard, 1st Earl of Suffolk. She married the 3rd Earl of Essex in 1606 and was divorced in 1613 when she married her lover, Robert Carr, Earl of Somerset. Their part in poisoning Sir Thomas Overbury came to light in 1615. Both were found guilty but pardoned, although imprisoned in the Tower until 1622 and after in the country.

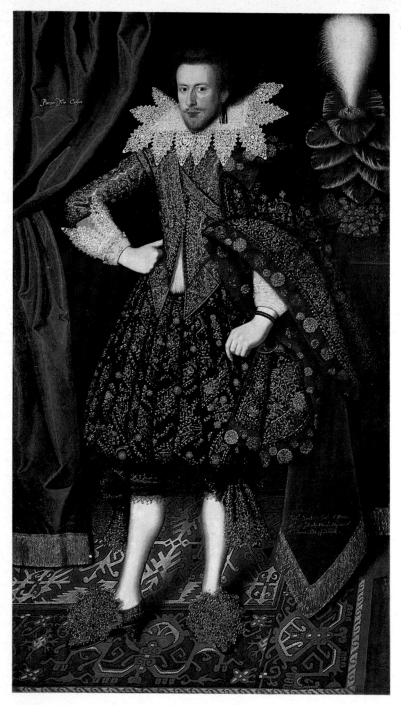

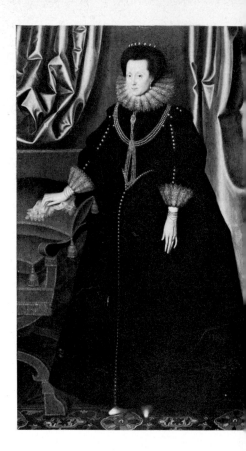

THE REDLYNCH
LONG GALLERY SET

circa 1614

Attributed. A series of seven full lengths of ladies, possibly commissioned about 1614 as a single decorative scheme to commemorate the marriage of Elizabeth Cecil to Thomas Howard, 1st Earl of Berkshire. As a group they are Larkin's masterpiece and the most important series of portraits to survive unbroken from this period.

William Larkin *Edward Sackville, 4th Earl of Dorset* (no. 128)

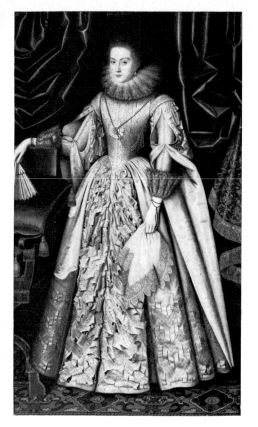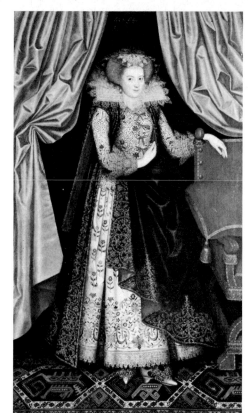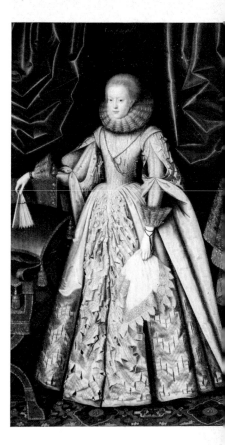

133 (left)

Elizabeth Drury, Countess of Exeter

The Executors of the Estate of the late Countess of Suffolk and Berkshire

Oil on canvas, 80 × 46 inches

Elizabeth (1579–1654), daughter of Sir William Drury of Hawsted, was wife of William, 2nd Earl of Exeter and was mother of the bride, Elizabeth Cecil.

134 (left centre)

Diana Cecil, Countess of Oxford

The Executors of the Estate of the late Countess of Suffolk and Berkshire

Oil on canvas, 80 × 46 inches

Twin sister of Anne (no. 136). Diana (*died* 1654) was the daughter of William Cecil, 2nd Earl of Exeter, and married Henry de Vere, Earl of Oxford in 1624.

135 (right centre)

Dorothy St. John, Lady Cary

The Executors of the Estate of the late Countess of Suffolk and Berkshire

Oil on canvas, 80 × 46 inches

136 (right)

Anne Cecil, Countess of Stamford

The Executors of the Estate of the late Countess of Suffolk and Berkshire

Oil on canvas, 80 × 46 inches

Anne Cecil was Diana's twin (no. 134) and younger sister of the bride. She married Henry Grey, 1st Earl of Stamford in 1620.

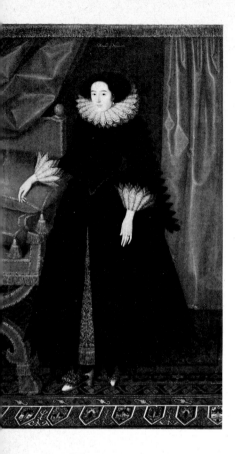
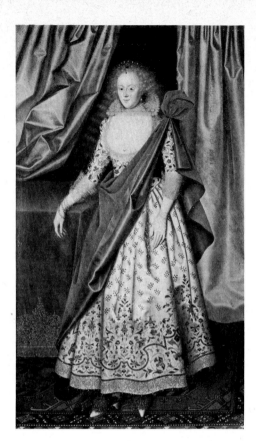
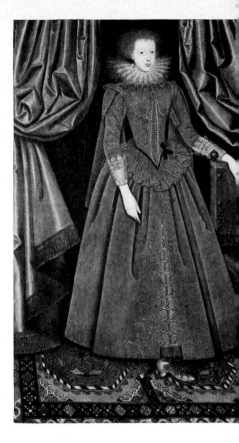

137 (left)

Elizabeth Howard, Duchess of Newcastle

The Executors of the Estate of the late Countess of Suffolk
and Berkshire
Oil on canvas, 80 × 48 inches

Elizabeth Bassett (*died* 1643), married William Cavendish, 1st
Duke of Newcastle married about 1618.

138 (centre)

Lady Isabella Rich

The Executors of the Estate of the late Countess of Suffolk
and Berkshire
Oil on canvas, 80 × 48 inches

Presumably Isabella Cope (*died* 1655), heiress of Sir Walter
Cope, who married Henry Rich in or before 1616. He later
became Baron Kensington and Earl Holland.

139 (right)

Catherine Rich, Countess of Suffolk

The Executors of the Estate of the late Countess of Suffolk
and Berkshire
Oil on canvas, 80 × 47 inches

Catherine Rich, Countess of Suffolk (born after 1583 and still
living in 1638) was widow of Robert, 2nd Baron Rich and
daughter and co-heir of Sir Henry Knyrett of Charlton. She
married Thomas Howard, Earl of Suffolk in or before 1583 as
his second wife. She had smallpox in 1619 'which spoiled that
good face of hers, which had brought to others much misery
and to herself greatness which ended with much unhappiness'.

VI

Elizabethan and Jacobean Melancholy

' . . . sigh a note and sing a note . . . with your hat penthouse — like o'er the shop of your eyes, with your arms crossed on your thin-belly doublet, like a rabbit on a spit . . .'

Don Armado 'besieged by sable-coloured melancholy'
SHAKESPEARE *Love's Labour Lost*

Through a renaissance revaluation the melancholic humour became the one to cultivate, being an indication of intellectual prowess in scholarship, philosophy and poetry. Robert Burton's *Anatomy of Melancholy* (1621), which summed up a movement which was first imported into England from Italy in the late eighties, states that 'melancholy men of all others are most witty'. Lovers were always supposed to be melancholic and many portraits depict young gallants in the attributes of a melancholy lover (*e.g.* nos. 141, 142 and 143). But the whole problem, here simplified, is more complicated. In the nineties people begin to be recorded in their portraits as human beings with psychological moods as against the icons of an earlier period. These events coincide with the play of the humours and the general mood of gloom which permeates the late Elizabethan and Jacobean society.

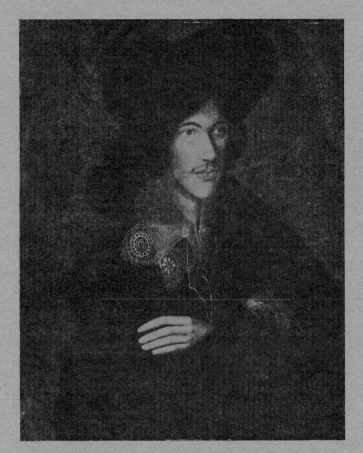

140

ARTIST UNKNOWN *circa* 1595

John Donne

The Marquess of Lothian
Oil on panel, $28\frac{1}{2} \times 24$ inches

Donne is here casting himself in the role of a melancholy lover.
A Latin inscription, a parody of the psalms, implores his lady
to whom he owes a saint-like devotion, to lighten the shadows
which envelope his love-sick misery: *Illumina tenebras nostras
domina*. Donne has all the usual trappings: a large hat with a
floppy black brim, arms folded across his chest, black dress, his
collar negligently left undone. Later in life melancholy took
its religious form and in his *Corona* of Sonnets he offers to God:

> . . . this crown of prayers and praise,
> Weav'd in my low devout melancholie.

141

ISAAC OLIVER

A Melancholy Young Man *circa* 1595

Her Majesty The Queen
Miniature, $4\frac{5}{8} \times 3\frac{1}{4}$ inches

The identity of the sitter is not known although in the 18th
century it was published as Sir Philip Sidney. He may
be compared with the figure of Democritus of Abdera as
he appears on the engraved title page of Burton's *Anatomy*
(no. 144) contemplating 'the vanity and fopperies of the time,
to see men so empty of all virtuous action'. Sir John Davies
describes a fashionable melancholic gallant thus:

> See yonder melancholy gentleman,
> Which hood-wink'd with his hat, alone doth sit!
> Thinke what he thinks, and tell me if you can,
> What great affaires troubles his little wit.
> He thinks not of the warre 'twixt France and Spaine,
> But he doth seriously bethinke him whether
> Of the gull'd people he be most esteem'd
> For his long cloake or for his great black feather,
> By which each gull is now a gallant deem'd,
> Or of a journey he deliberates,
> To Paris-garden, Cock-pit or the Play:
> Or how to steale a dog he meditates,
> Or what he shall unto his mistress say . . .

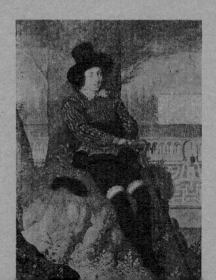

142

ISAAC OLIVER

Edward Herbert, 1st Baron Herbert of Cherbury
circa 1610–15

The Earl of Powis
Miniature, 9 × 7⅛ inches
Illustrated in colour on the front cover

Lord Herbert is here the melancholy knight, seeking the solace of the greenwood tree close to a little trickling stream. Burton (no 144) says 'What is more pleasant than to walk alone in some solitary grove, betwixt Wood and Water, by a Brook side, to meditate upon some delightsome and pleasant subject . . . A most incomparable delight it is so to melancholize, and build castles in the air . . .' The shield contains an *impresa* and the motto *Magica Sympathia* referring to the doctrine of sympathetic magic. (See no. 56).

143

ARTIST UNKNOWN

Robert Sydney, 1st Earl of Leicester *circa* 1585

J. J. W. Salmond Esq;
on loan to Lancaster House, Ministry of Works
Oil on canvas, 80 × 42 inches

This picture was included in the 1588 inventory of Sydney's uncle, Robert Dudley, Earl of Leicester. It is one of the earliest portraits of an Englishman in a melancholic pose (see no. 109).

144

ROBERT BURTON

The Anatomy of Melancholy 1628 edition

The British Museum Library

Burton's *Anatomy* summed up the whole 'melancholy movement' dealing with every aspect from love-sickness to total madness. The book shows the title-page of the 1628 edition which is a useful visual index of melancholic poses. Top centre, Democritus of Abdera, the laughing philosopher, may be compared with no. 141. Centre left is a melancholic lover with floppy hat and crossed arms.

145

JOHN MILTON

Poems of Mr. John Milton, both English and Latin, compos'd at several times 1645

Milton's *Il Penseroso* published in this volume is the poetic quintessence of the mood and imagery of *melancholia*. The book is open at a passage which reads almost like an iconographic programme for Lord Herbert's miniature (see no. 142).

146

RICHARD HAYDOCKE

Tracte containing the Artes of curious Paintinge, Carvinge, Buildinge, Oxford 1598

The British Museum Library

A translation of Giovanni Lomazzo's *Trattato dell'arte della pittura* (1584). Through this book ideas of mannerist art theory reached England. It has an important preface mentioning many Elizabethan painters and referring to the fact that examples of the works of the best foreign masters may already be seen in English collections.

ISAAC OLIVER

circa 1556(?)–1617

French born painter who came to England as a child and was trained as a miniaturist by Nicholas Hilliard. He probably travelled in the Low Countries in 1588 and was in Venice in 1596 (see no. 148). Oliver married Marcus Gheeraerts' sister Sara. Together the two artists achieved a total change of style and mood in painting in the nineties. The sunshine of Hilliard's miniatures is replaced by the shadow of Oliver's, and colours once pink, yellow, green and blue become brown, black, purple and puce. We know he painted 'greate pictures' in oil for Henry Prince of Wales although identification of them is speculative.

ELIZABETH I *circa* 1590–1600 (see no. 79).

147

An Unknown Man aged 27 1590

Victoria and Albert Museum
Miniature, $2\frac{1}{8} \times 1\frac{3}{4}$ inches

An example of the chiaroscuro style that Oliver brought to miniature painting.

148

Sir Arundell Talbot 1596

Victoria and Albert Museum
Miniature, $2\frac{3}{4} \times 2\frac{1}{8}$ inches

Evidence of Oliver's visit to Italy as the back is inscribed with the artist's name, the place, Venice, and the day, May 13th 1596. Nothing is known of a 'Sir Arundell Talbot'.

A MELANCHOLY YOUNG MAN, *circa* 1595 (see no. 141).
EDWARD HERBERT, 1ST BARON HERBERT OF CHERBURY, *circa* 1610–15 (see no. 142).
HENRY, PRINCE OF WALES, *circa* 1610 (see nos. 180–1).

149 (left)

Self Portrait *circa* 1595

The Earl of Derby, on loan to Manchester City Art Gallery
Miniature, $2 \times 2\frac{1}{2}$ inches

An excellent instance of Oliver's portrait style which shows the influence of Flemish portrature of the late eighties.

150

Adoration of the Magi

British Museum, Department of Prints and Drawings
Drawing, $9 \times 6\frac{5}{8}$ inches

A typical instance of Oliver's style in subject drawing showing heavily the influence of Parmigianino. Oliver probably brought back from Italy a collection of Italian engravings.

151

The Baziliωlogia 1618

The National Portrait Gallery

A series of engraved portraits of monarchs from William I to James I. This publication had printed predecessors back to Rastell's *Pastyme of People* (1529). It was part of a literature, European in its extent, of engraved books of portraits which owed much to the publications of Paolo Giovio. The early kings are mythical, some adapted from Domenico Custos' engravings of the Kings of Naples. Painted sets of kings and queens were typical long-gallery decoration.

152

The Herωologia 1620

The National Portrait Gallery

Henry Holland's second venture, this time based on Verheiden's compilation of Protestant theologians and worthies published in The Hague in 1602. Holland's collection is of reformers and opponents of the Pope and the engravings are by Willem and Magdalena van de Passe. It is important as Holland specifically states that the portraits were taken from oil paintings and he excluded those whose portrait he could not find. A copy inscribed *P. Mariette* 1682 contains notes on the source of some of the portraits and on the artists (see no. 28).

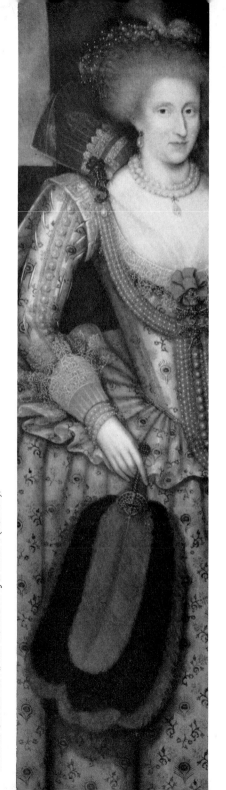

Marcus Gheeraerts: detail from *Anne of Denmark* (no. 160).

VII

Marcus Gheeraerts

Such was his beauty that the force of light,
Whose knowledge teacheth wonders infinite,
The strength of number and proportion,
Nature had placed in it to make it known
Art was her daughter

GEORGE CHAPMAN *Hero and Leander*

MARCUS GHEERAERTS THE YOUNGER
flourished 1561–1636

The most important painter working in England between *circa* 1590 and *circa* 1620. He was brought over as a child from Flanders and belonged to the Flemish exile group of artists living in London. His sister married Isaac Oliver and he himself married John de Critz's sister, Magdalena. He seems to have travelled abroad sometime in the late eighties as his style was fundamentally influenced by the new Antwerp School and its principal exponent, Frans Pourbus. Gheeraerts, backed by powerful patronage, swiftly became the most fashionable painter of the day. By 1592, when the Queen sat to him, his position was assured and it remained unchallenged until the close of the second decade of the new century when changing tastes and the arrival of new artists from abroad, such as van Somer, resulted in a fall from favour. At his peak he produced some of the most tender and touching characterisations in Elizabethan and Jacobean painting. With his brother-in-law, Isaac Oliver, he was the prime interpreter of the new mood of fantasy, introspection and melancholy that pervaded fashionable society from the beginning of the nineties.

A large *oeuvre* can confidently be assembled around Gheeraerts. Eight signed pictures are known, three documented and twenty-two bearing identical forms of inscription recording date, age of sitter, etc. A further twenty can also be certainly accepted as from his brush.

ELIZABETH I, 1592 ? (See no. 78).

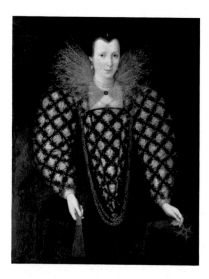

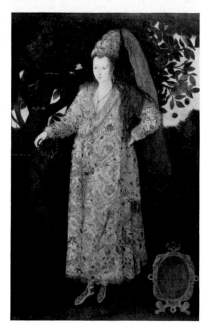

153

Lady in Fancy Dress *circa* 1590–1600

Her Majesty The Queen
Oil on panel, $85\frac{1}{2} \times 53\frac{1}{2}$ inches

Inscribed. The lady is disguised as a Persian Virgin, a costume derived from the figure of a *Virgo Persica* in Boissard's *Habitus Variarum Orbis gentium* Antwerp, 1581. The general theme is that of love-lorn melancholy but the specific allusions are extremely cryptic. She is in the act of crowning a weeping stag with a chaplet of pansies and she is seeking the shade of the greenwood tree. The rambling sonnet in the cartouche (which is an excellent example of Gheeraerts script) is full of sad complaining: of 'wronges', 'cruelty unkinde', 'melancholy teares', 'sighes unknowne' and 'harmes'. Her only hope was 'in this goodly tree, which I did plant in love' but even the fruit of this has gone to others:

> *My Musique maybe plaintes, my physique teares*
> *If this be all the fruite my love tree beares.*

154 (left)

Unknown Lady 1593

E. Bullivant, Esq.
Oil on panel, 45×37 inches
Inscribed.

155
Thomas Lee 1594

Captain Loel Guinness, on loan to the Tate Gallery
Oil on canvas, 98 × 62 inches

Inscribed. One of a series of Gheeraerts full-length canvases once at the house of his patron, Sir Henry Lee (see no. 54). Lee is disguised as an Irish Knight with bare legs to facilitate his progress through the watery bogs of Ireland. The costume is based on an engraving in Boissard's *Habitus variarum orbis gentium*, Antwerp, 1581 (see also no. 153).

Thomas Lee, Sir Henry's wayward nephew, sought his fortunes in Ireland. Later he took part in the Essex rebellion and was executed at Tyburn.

156
Barbara Gamage, Lady Sidney and her Children 1596

The Viscount De L'Isle
Oil on canvas, 80 × 102½ inches

Documented. In the 18th century there existed a letter from the sitter's husband directing his wife to settle her account with Gheeraerts 'for her picture and the Childrens'.

Barbara Gamage (died 1621) married Robert Sidney, later Earl of Leicester, in 1584. The children are: William (Sir William Sidney died 1613), Robert (later the 2nd Earl), Mary (married Sir Robert Wroth), Catherine (married Sir Lewis Mansel, Bt), Elizabeth and Philippa (married Sir John Hobart). Robert Sidney was created Earl of Leicester in 1621, having been knighted by 1596, anc created successively Baron Sidney of Penshurst 1603 and Viscount De L'Isle 1605.

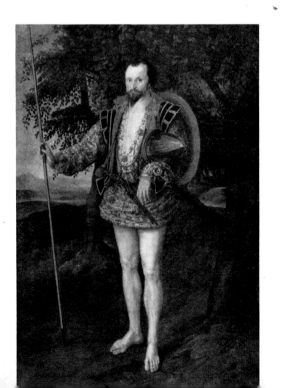

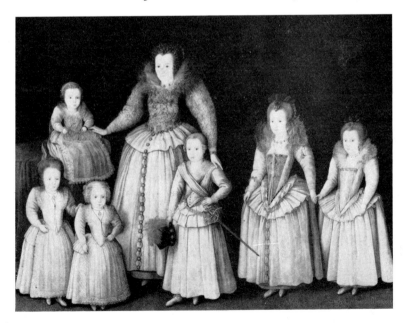

157

Robert Devereux, 2nd Earl of Essex *circa* 1596

The Duke of Bedford and the Trustees of the Bedford Settled Estates
Oil on canvas, 84 × 50 inches

Attributed. With no. 78, Gheeraerts' masterpiece from the
nineties painted shortly after the return of Essex from his
expedition to Cadiz. The city itself can be seen in the distance
right aflame. This is the prime original from life of which many
other smaller versions were painted by the studio. (See no. 57.)

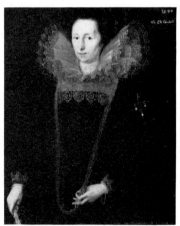

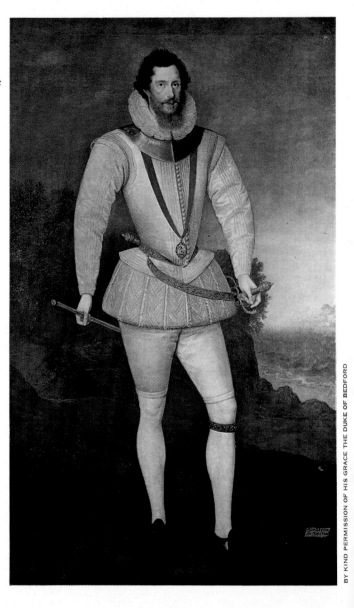

158

Called **Mary Tufton, 1st Viscountess Dunbar** 1599

J. R. Chichester Constable, Esq.
Oil on panel, 35 × 29 inches

Attributed. This is a typical instance of a Gheeraerts
three-quarter length of lady from the nineties. Mary Lady
Dunbar (died 1659) was daughter of Sir John Tufton and
married Henry Constable, 1st Viscount Constable in or before
1612. The portrait depicts too old a lady at too early a date
and probably represents the Viscount's mother, Margaret,
daughter of Sir William Dormer.

BY KIND PERMISSION OF HIS GRACE THE DUKE OF BEDFORD

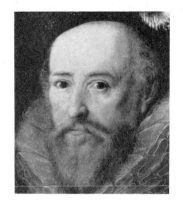

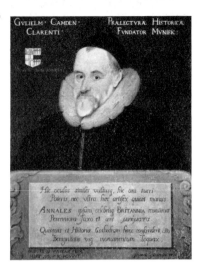

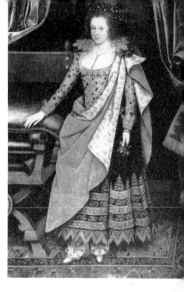

159 (right, detail)

Sir Henry Lee 1600

Hugh Wontner, Esq.
Oil on canvas, 45 × 36 inches

Inscribed. Lee was one of Gheeraerts' major patrons.
For a biography see no. 54.

160 (below)

Anne of Denmark *circa* 1605–10

The Duke of Bedford and the Trustees of the Bedford Settled Estates
Oil on canvas, 84 × 50 inches

Attributed. Gheeraerts was painter to the new Queen, Anne of Denmark, and this canvas was presumably painted to give to her great friend, Lucy Harington, Countess of Bedford, (see no. 176). Gheeraerts establishes a totally different mood for Anne compared with the icons of majesty that were manufactured for the old Queen. Anne is apotheosised more as the lady than as the queen.
For Anne see no. 175.

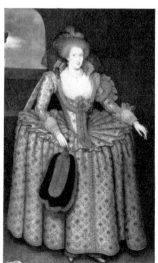

161 (above)

William Camden 1609

The Bodleian Library, Oxford
Oil on panel, 30 × 23 inches

Signed. Presented to the Schools by Degory Wheare, first Camden Professor. William Camden (1551–1623) was the great antiquarian and historian of the age. His two most-important works are *Britannia* (1586) and the *Annales* of Elizabeth's reign (1615).

162 (above, right)

Frances Howard, Duchess of Richmond 1611

The Viscount Cowdray
Oil on canvas, 81 × 51 inches

Attributed. Frances Howard (died 1639) was daughter of Thomas, 1st Viscount Howard of Bindon. Ludovic Stuart, Duke of Richmond and Lennox, was her third husband. She married firstly Henry Pranell, and secondly Edward Seymour, 1st Earl of Hertford.

163

Called **Elizabeth, Queen of Bohemia** 1612

Private Collection
Oil on panel, 43 × 32½ inches
Attributed.

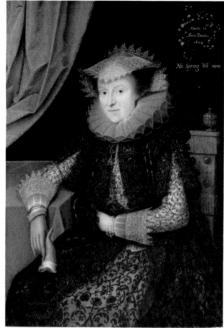

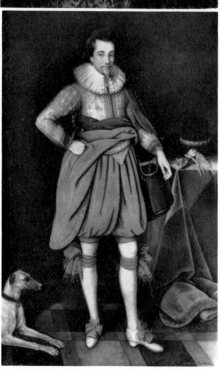

164

Sir John Kennedy 1614

The Duke of Bedford and the Trustees of the Bedford Settled Estates
Oil on canvas, $78\frac{1}{2} \times 45\frac{1}{2}$ inches

Inscribed. The background right contains a view of a long gallery showing how pictures used to be hung, including the use of curtains drawn over them. References in the literature of the period to curtains being drawn aside are fairly common. Sir John Kennedy of Barn Elms (died 1614) was a Scot who came south with James I and married the heiress, Elizabeth Brydges (no. 116). Kennedy was already married and later drove his new wife from the house with great brutality.

165 (above left)

Mary Throckmorton, Lady Scudamore 1614/5

The National Portrait Gallery, on loan to the Tate Gallery
Oil on panel, $45 \times 32\frac{1}{2}$ inches

Inscribed. The inscription records the date March 12th 1614 when Lady Scudamore's son, John married Elizabeth Porter. Above a garland of spring flowers encircle the motto: *No spring till now.*

Mary Throckmorton (died 1632) was the daughter of Sir Thomas Throckmorton of Coss Court, Tentworth. She married firstly Sir Thomas Baskerville (died 1596) and secondly, in 1599, Sir John Scudamore of Holme Lacy. In 1609 she complained to Lord Salisbury that her father-in-law had turned her out of her house and her husband ill-treated her.

166 (left)

Sir Thomas Parker *circa* 1620

The National Trust, Saltram House
Oil on canvas, 84×53 inches

Attributed. Sir Thomas Parker, presumably the second son of John Parker recorded as aged 26 in 1620. His eldest brother was the ancestor of the Lords Boringdon and Morley who built Saltram House.

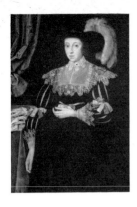

167 (above)

Anne, Lady Fanshawe *circa* 1627–28

The London Borough of Barking
Oil on panel, 43 × 31 inches

Attributed. Cf. no. 168. Anne Alington (1607–1628) was the first wife of Thomas, 1st Viscount Fanshawe. She died in childbirth a year later, aged 21.

168 (below)

Anne Hale, Mrs Hoskins 1629

Private collection
Oil on panel, 44 × 32½ inches

Signed. Anne Hale (?1609–51) was daughter of William Hale of King's Walden and wife of Charles Hoskins of Barrow Green.

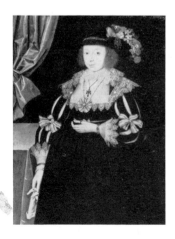

JOHN DE CRITZ 1552(?)–1642

With Scrots the most enigmatic of the painters dealt with in this exhibition. The few obliquely documented items give us little real clue as to his *oeuvre*. He came to England as a child from the Low Countries and was patronised by Sir Francis Walsingham, who sent him to France and probably Italy. His sisters married the Gheeraerts, father and son. In 1605 he became jointly, with Peake, Sergeant Painter.

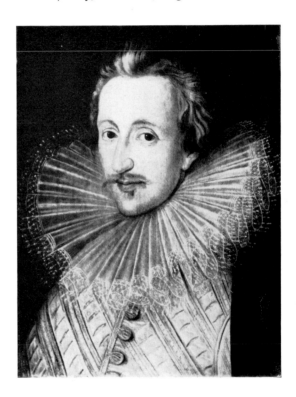

169

Sir Philip Sidney *circa* 1585

The Lady Cobbold
Oil on panel, 20 × 16 inches

Attributed. One of three versions of this portrait probably by De Critz. It was engraved in 1620 in the *Herωologia*, and some late 17th-century marginalia state it is after De Critz. A drawing by Vertue after a drawing by De Critz of a three-quarter-length version of this portrait also exists (Warren Lowenhaupt Collection, Yale) (see no. 55).

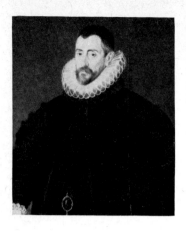 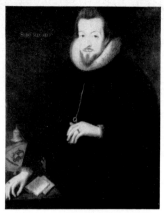 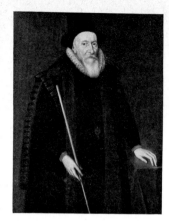 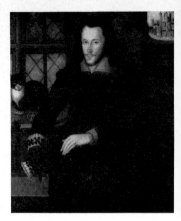

170 (above, left)

Sir Francis Walsingham *circa* 1585

National Portrait Gallery
Oil on panel, 30 × 25 inches

Attributed. One of the best versions of this portrait which on account of Walsingham's patronage is reasonably attributed to De Critz.

Sir Francis Walsingham (1530?–1590), Elizabeth's secretary of state, was concerned primarily with foreign affairs. His influence was used to further the Protestant cause; he maintained a brilliant intelligence network which unravelled numerous Catholic plots against the Queen.

171 (above, centre left)

Robert Cecil, 1st Earl of Salisbury 1602

The National Portrait Gallery
Oil on panel, 35½ × 28⅞ inches

Attributed. This is one of many versions of this portrait painted by De Critz, for Cecil, being a short hunch-back, only ever sat for his portrait once. Payments for four by De Critz in 1607 are in the Hatfield House accounts. The earliest version is dated 1599.

Robert Cecil, 1st Earl of Salisbury (1563–1612) succeeded his father Lord Burghley as chief minister of Elizabeth I. He successfully engineered the accession of James I, whose minister he also became.

172 (above, centre right)

Thomas Sackville, 1st Earl of Dorset 1601

National Portrait Gallery
Oil on panel, 43½ × 34½ inches

Attributed. It is attributed on the grounds of its relationship to no. 171. Several other versions exist, the original, also dated 1601, probably being that at Knole, the family home.

Thomas Sackville, Earl of Dorset (1536–1608) collaborated, in 1561, in the authorship of the tragedy *Gorboduc*. His career in later life was a distinguished one culminating in his appointment as Lord Treasurer, 1599. He presided at the trial of Essex and was commissioner for peace with Spain, 1604.

173 (above, right)

Henry Wriothesley, 3rd Earl of Southampton 1603

The Duke of Buccleuch and Queensbury
Oil on canvas, 41½ × 34¼ inches

Attributed. Compare the arrangement of the cloak and hands with no. 171. The portrait commemorates Southampton's imprisonment in the Tower for his part in the Essex rebellion. The Tower is top right with the Thames, on which swans float, before it. See no. 86.

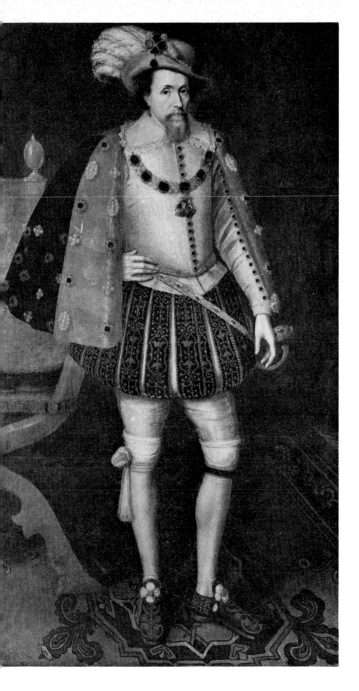

174

James I *circa* 1605

J. R. More-Molyneux, Esq.
Oil on canvas, 79 × 46½ inches

Attributed. This is a good example of the first portrait type of James to be produced in his reign. De Critz as Serjeant Painter can reasonably be associated with its production and payments exist in accounts to De Critz for such portraits. Very many other versions of varying size exist.

Sir Anthony Weldon records that 'James could never be brought to sit for the taking of that [picture], which is the reason of so few good pieces of him.' In these portraits the jewels in the hat alternate between three legendary jewels of the crown, the Mirror of Great Britain, the Feather and the Three Brothers. In this he wears the Mirror of Great Britain, a jewel made for James to symbolise the Union of the Kingdoms in 1604:

'item, a greate and riche jewell of gould, called the MIRROR OF GREATE BRITTAINE, containing one very faire table diamonde, one very faire table-rubie, two other large diamonds cutt lozengwise, the one of them called the stone of the letter H. of SCOTLANDE, garnished with small diamonds, two rounde pearles fixed, and one fayre diamonde cut in fourcetts, bought of Sancy.'

The famous Sancy diamond was sold to James in 1604 in time for him to wear it in his hat at his coronation entry on March 21st.

James VI of Scotland and I of England (1566–1625) succeeded Elizabeth I in 1603. A man of great learning, he was the exponent of an extreme doctrine of kingship, the Divine Right of Kings, which led him into difficulties with Parliament. He pursued a conciliatory foreign policy as the Solomon of Europe uniting rival religious camps through marriages. He showed no real interest in the visual arts.

175

Anne of Denmark 1605

J. R. More-Molyneux, Esq.
Oil on canvas, 79 × 46½ inches

Attributed. Companion piece to no. 174, which entry
consult for reasons of attribution. As in the case of James other
versions of varying size exist.

Anne of Denmark (1574–1619) was daughter of Frederick II of
Denmark and married James in 1589. She had pronounced
artistic tastes both literary and visual. Anne chose for her own
painters Isaac Oliver and Marcus Gheeraerts and later, in 1617,
patronised van Somer (see no. 186). For her Ben Jonson and
Inigo Jones inaugurated the famous series of masques (see nos.
60, 61 and 182–4) which began in 1605 with the *Maske of
Blacknesse*. Inigo Jones began the Queen's House,
Greenwich for Anne.

176

Lucy Harrington, Countess of Bedford 1606

*The Duke of Bedford and the Trustees of the Bedford Settled
Estate*
Oil on canvas, 80¼ × 48 inches

Attributed. The elongated spidery fingers seem typical of
De Critz. One of a series of three canvases depicting ladies in
their masque costumes designed by Inigo Jones for Jonson's
Hymenaei:

'The Ladies *attyre* was wholly new, for the invention, and full
of glorie; as having in it the most true impression of a *celestrall*
figure: the upper part of *white* cloth of silver, wrought with
IVNOES *birds* and *fruits*; a loose undergarment, full gather'd,
of carnation, strip't with *silver*, and parted with a golden *zone*:
beneath that, another flowing garment, of *watchet* cloth of
silver, lac'd with gold; through all of which though they were
round and swelling, there yet appeared some touch of their
delicat *lineaments*, preserving the *sweetnesse* of proportion,
and expressing it selfe beyond expression.'

Lucy Harrington, Countess of Bedford (died 1627) was a great
friend of Anne of Denmark (no. 175) and with her led all court
revels. She lived extravagantly and was a patron of poets,
including Jonson. She had a passion for portraits and
accumulated a great collection at Woburn, much of it still there.

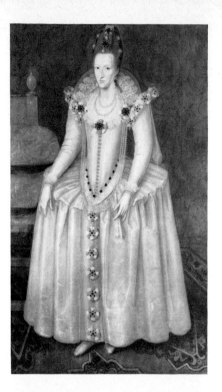

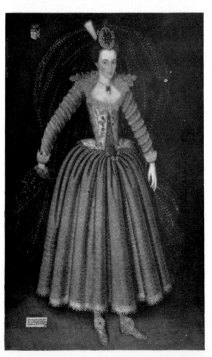

78

VIII

Epilogue

Picture is the invention of heaven,
the most ancient and most akin to
Nature. It is itself a silent work . . .
yet it doth so enter and penetrate
the inmost affection . . . as
sometimes to o'ercome the power
of speech and oratory.

BEN JONSON

A CHRONICLE OF EVENTS 1603–1620

1603	Accession of James VI of Scotland as James I of England
1604	England makes peace with Spain
1605	The first of the Stuart masques, Ben Jonson's *Masque of Blacknesse*, designed by Inigo Jones The Gunpowder Plot
1610	Henry created Prince of Wales
1612	Death of Henry, Prince of Wales
1613	Elizabeth marries Frederick, Elector Palatine
1616	Death of William Shakespeare
1617	**Death of Isaac Oliver** (no. 178) **Paul van Somer paints Anne of Denmark** (no. 186)
1617–23	Negotiations with Spain for the marriage of Prince Charles to the Infanta
1619	**Death of Nicholas Hilliard** (no. 177) Death of Anne of Denmark Whitehall Banqueting House burnt: Inigo Jones begins work on a new one

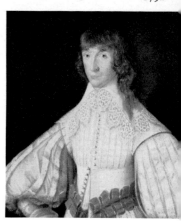

177
Nicholas Hilliard's Will 1618

Principal Probate Registry, Somerset House

Hilliard made his will on December 24th 1618 and died probably early in January 1619. Two years before Hilliard had been imprisoned for debt in Ludgate. His will leaves little, the residue going to his son, the miniaturist, Lawrence.

178 (below)
Isaac Oliver's Will 1617

Principal Probate Registry, Somerset House

In this Oliver left to his miniaturist son Peter 'all my drawings allready finished and unfinished and lymning pictures, be they historyes, storyes, or anything of lymning whatsoever of my owne hande worke as yet unfinished'.

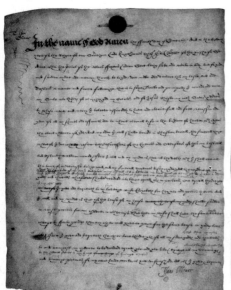
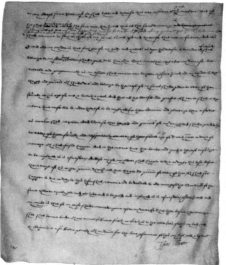
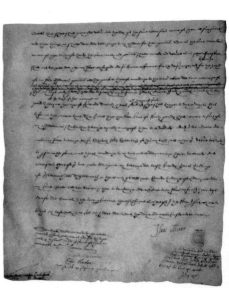

179b · 179c

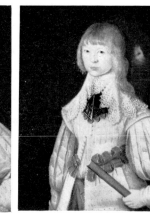

179

FOLLOWER OF PEAKE *circa* 1630

a) **Unknown Youth** *circa* 1630

Private collection
Oil on canvas, $28\frac{1}{4} \times 25$

b) **Unknown Youth** *circa* 1630

Private collection
Oil on canvas, $28\frac{1}{2} \times 25\frac{3}{4}$

c) **Unknown Youth** *circa* 1630

Private collection
Oil on canvas, $28\frac{1}{2} \times 22\frac{1}{4}$

Despite the changes in taste at court the Hilliard tradition continued elsewhere up to the outbreak of the Civil War. These paintings show the high standard that could be maintained by traditional craftsmen.

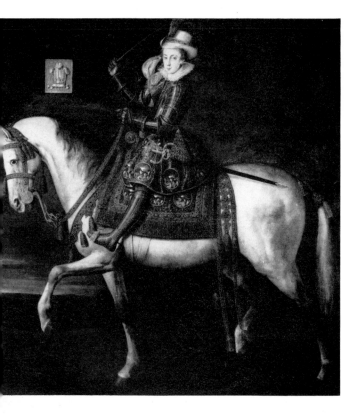

180

ISAAC OLIVER

Henry, Prince of Wales, *circa* 1610

Mrs P. A. Tritton
Oil on canvas, 90 × 86 inches

Attributed. The earliest large-scale equestrian portrait of a royal personage in English painting. Inspired probably by paintings by Clouet of the Valois kings on horseback, it is painted in the manner of the Venetians.

Prince Henry during the short period from his creation as Prince of Wales (1610) until his death (1612) attempted to achieve an aesthetic revolution. He was the first royal person to collect works of art, which included renaissance bronzes and Venetian paintings. Inigo Jones was his surveyor and a Florentine architect, Constantino dei Servi, entered his service. In April 1611 he opened negotiations to persuade Miereveldt to be his court painter. This new baroque image went hand-in-hand with a revival of chivalry (see nos. 60-1). His death retarded the aesthetic revolution a decade.

181

ISAAC OLIVER

Henry, Prince of Wales, *circa* 1610

Her Majesty The Queen
Miniature, $5\frac{1}{8} \times 5$ inches

In the collection of Charles I, where it was described as 'The biggest limned picture that was made of Prince Henry'. The military nature of the portrait gives further evidence of the part Prince Henry played in the cult of chivalry (see no. 61).

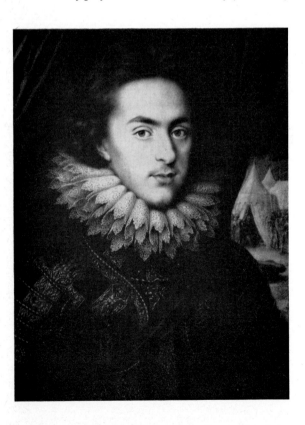

INIGO JONES

Inigo Jones was already over thirty when he entered royal service as designer of court fêtes for Anne of Denmark. Although he had travelled abroad late in Elizabeth's reign there is little in his early designs that make them more than a spectacular continuation of late Elizabethan revels. Aubrey records that Inigo drew the castles of England for James I and his designs link him decisively to the world of late Elizabethan chivalry (see nos. 60-1). In 1613 he went to Italy in the train of Arundel which had an immense impact. On his return he takes up his position as arbiter of taste at court for twenty-five years promoting the new palladian style and producing the masques. As a man trained in the tradition of the full range of the Vitruvian desciplines as understood by the renaissance the 'architect' was a universal man operating in the mechanical-mathematical sphere whether it be a house, fortifications or sets and machines for a play or masque.

182

The Release of the Daughters of the Morn 1611

The Trustees of the Chatsworth Settlement
Drawing, $18\frac{3}{4} \times 15\frac{1}{8}$ inches

Design for the final scene in the Queen's masque of *Love Freed from Ignorance and Folly* by Ben Jonson. The masquers, the eleven Daughters of the Morn released from the Prison of Night, can be seen descending in a cloud past the prison. No other drawing by Inigo quite so clearly demonstrates the duality of his mood: the goddesses are entirely Italianate, indeed Parmigianesque figures, in a renaissance cloud machine; but they descend past the entrance to a medieval castle complete with portcullis. The *Barriers* (nos. 60 and 61) and the *Masque of Oberon* show the same division of content. These were years of chivalrous revival which affected, for instance, architecture in the building of Bolsover.

183

A Prospect of Whitehall with the Banqueting House 1623

Private collection
Drawing, $15 \times 25\frac{1}{4}$ inches

Design for the opening scene in Jonson's *Time Vindicated*: 'the first that was discovered was a prospective of Whitehall with the Banqueting House'.

Whitehall Palace was the setting for nearly all the masques and plays embellished by Jones' designs. Elizabeth I had erected the first great *salle des fêtes* in 1581 in preparation for the visit of the French commissioners concerning her projected marriage to the Duke of Anjou. This building, which was a strictly temporary structure, lasted until 1606 when James I ordered the demolition of 'the old rotten, sleight builded Banqueting house' and a new hall was constructed under the direction of Sir David Conyngham. In January 1619 this burned to the ground and in expectation of the completion of the match between Prince Charles and the Spanish Infanta, a new ceremonial hall was begun instantly under the direction of Inigo Jones. Work on this came to a standstill in the late 1620's and the final finishing touches were added over a decade later. Few masques were in fact ever staged in the Banqueting House for fear of ruining Rubens' ceiling paintings and it was finally abandoned in 1635. As a building the Banqueting House epitomises an artistic revolution and remains Inigo's supreme statement of the principles of Palladio.

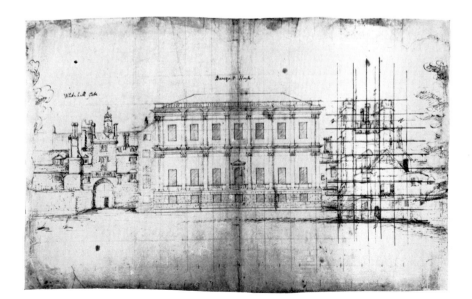

184
The House of Oceanus

The Trustees of the Chatsworth Settlement
Drawing, $21\frac{3}{8} \times 17\frac{1}{8}$ inches

Designed for Ben Jonson's *Neptunes Triumph for the Reformed Albion* to celebrate Prince Charles's return from Spain. It was never performed due to a diplomatic impasse and the scenery was re-used in 1625 for *The Fortunate Isles and their Union*. The description is as follows:

'All, that is discovered of a *Scene*, are two erected *Pillars*, dedicated to *Neptune*, with this inscription upon the one, NEP. RED. on the other SEC. IOV.' 'Which done, the first prospective of a maritime Palace, or the house of Oceanus is discovered, with loud Musique.'

This is the earliest surviving drawing which shows quite clearly the use of perspective in staging which Jones first introduced in 1605 in the *Maske of Blacknesse*. The masques with their picture-frame staging taught people to look at pictures in their frames in the same terms, those of aesthetic depth.

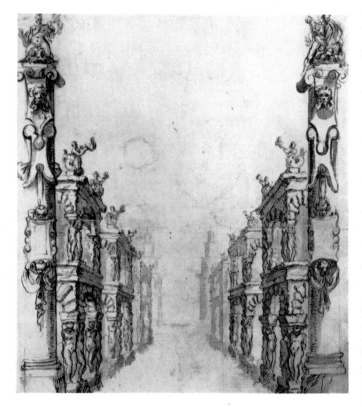

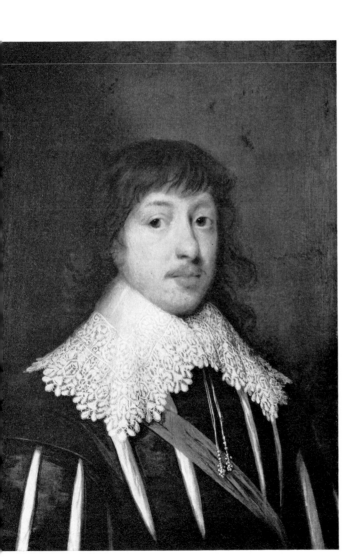

CORNELIUS JOHNSON 1593–1661

Painter whose work is outside the scope of this exhibition but acts as a link transmuting the Gheeraerts tradition under the impact of Van Dyck. He was directly connected with the Gheeraerts-Oliver circle through Oliver's marriage to Elizabeth Russell. Johnson was brother-in-law of Nicobius Russell, jeweller to James I. Johnson possibly trained under Gheeraerts.

185 (left)
Unknown Gentleman 1629

The Tate Gallery
Oil on panel, $17\frac{1}{2} \times 12\frac{1}{2}$ inches

A typical instance of Johnson's work showing the influence of Gheeraerts on his early style.

PAUL VAN SOMER *circa* 1577/8–1622

Netherlandish painter who came to England by 1616. He brought the new, more robust style of Netherlandish painting in its pre-Rubens tradition. Although not a painter of great quality his concept of Anne of Denmark (no. 186) painted in 1617 epitomised the oncoming revolution in painting.

186
Anne of Denmark 1617

Sir Gyles Isham, Bt.
Oil on canvas, 104 × 87 inches

This portrait embodies the elements of the revolution which overthrew the Elizabethan tradition and rendered obsolete too Gheeraerts and his followers. The Queen moves through an evening landscape in hunting attire, her dogs jumping at her skirt, a groom holding her horse. There is an Italian motto in the sky and Inigo Jones's new classical gateway to her palace of Oatlands is in the distance. It is conceived in terms of movement and depth as against the static and two-dimensional. For Anne's interest in the arts see no. 175.

ABRAHAM BLIJENBERGH

Antwerp painter who visited England probably about 1618.
Like Van Somer he brought the more robust style of the
Low Countries to a court still patronising Gheeraerts
and Larkin.

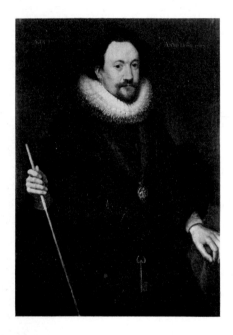

187

William Herbert, 3rd Earl of Pembroke 1617

The National Trust, Powis Castle
Oil on panel, 44 × 31 inches

Compare this with the portrait of his brother by Larkin
(no. 130) painted about five years before to understand the
impact of the new invasion of artists from the Low Countries.

The Earl of Pembroke (1580–1630) inherited a tradition of
literary patronage from his mother, Mary Sidney. He was
hailed as 'the greatest Maecenas to learned men of any peer of
his time or since'. His death is supposed to have been hastened
by 'pleasures of all kinds, almost in all excesses', and was in
debt £80,000.

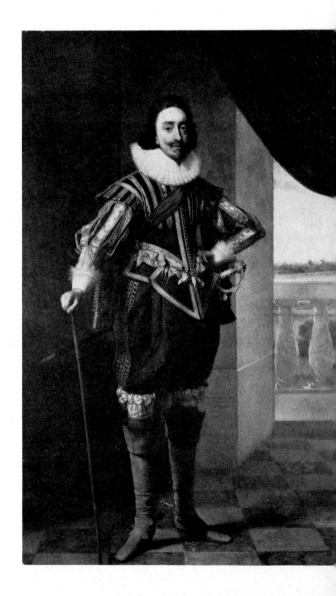

DANIEL MYTENS *circa* 1590–1647

Mytens was born in Delft and received his training as a painter at the Hague. By 1618 he was already in England receiving the patronage of Arundel. Soon after he received that of the Prince of Wales, who appointed him 'one of our picture drawers of our Chambers in ordinarie' for life. The advent of Mytens bringing the new incipient baroque quickly led to the old generation of Peake, de Critz and Gheeraerts being outmoded. Mytens fell from favour soon after the arrival of Van Dyck in 1632. Some time after this he returned to the Low Countries.

188 (left)
Charles I 1623

Her Majesty The Queen
Oil on canvas, 80⅜ × 51 inches

Probably painted soon after the Prince's return from Spain. Less than a decade separates this portrait from Peake's icons of the young Prince (see no. 113). Mytens stands at the beginning of the tremendous revolution in aesthetic taste which reached its climax in Van Dyck.

Charles I (1600–1649) inherited his brother's artistic tastes as well as his collection of Italian renaissance works of art. The visit to Spain to woo the Infanta enabled him to see the treasures of the Spanish royal collection. Philip IV presented Charles with Titian's *Venus of the Prado* and the Prince sat to Velasquez. Already he had acquired works by Rubens, Titian, Tintoretto and Holbein. In 1623 he acquired the Raphael cartoons.

189
Letter of Peter Paul Rubens to William Trumbull

Antwerp, September 13th 1621 (*contemporary copy*)
The Public Record Office

By 1621, the year this letter was written, Rubens was already patronised by the collectors of a new generation. The letter refers to a '*Hunt*' done on Sir Dudley Carleton's orders for Lord Danvers as a present to the Prince of Wales whose Gallery so far only included a *Judith and Hologernes* by Rubens. The *Hunt* was returned because the picture was studio work: 'he hath sent hither a peece scarce touched by his own hand, and the postures so forced, as the Prince will not admitt the picture to his gallerye' (Danvers to Carleton May 27th 1621). The letter closes mentioning the most important commission the Stuarts ever gave, the ceiling paintings of the new Whitehall Banqueting House. The paintings were not finally placed till 1635 but in response to this initial approach Rubens wrote 'I confess that I am, by natural instinct, better fitted to execute very large works than small curiosities'.

INDEX OF LENDERS